Start Your Own

NONPROFIT ORGANIZATION

Additional titles in *Entrepreneur's* Startup Series

Start Your Own

Entrepreneur
MAGAZINE'S

start up

Start Your Own

NONPROFIT ORGANIZATION

Your Step-by-Step Guide to Success

Entrepreneur Press and Cheryl Kimball

Ep
Entrepreneur
PRESS®

Entrepreneur Press, Publisher
Cover Design: Beth Hansen-Winter
Production and Composition: Eliot House Productions

This publication is designed to provide accurate and authoritative information in regard to
the subject matter covered. It is sold with the understanding that the publisher is not engaged
in rendering legal, accounting or other professional services. If legal advice or other expert
assistance is required, the services of a competent professional person should be sought.

Library of Congress Cataloging-in-Publication Data
    Kimball, Cheryl.
    Start your own nonprofit organization/by Entrepreneur Press and Cheryl Kimball.
        pages cm.—(Startup)
    Includes index.
    ISBN-13: 978-1-59918-527-9 (alk. paper)
    ISBN-10: 1-59918-527-X (alk. paper)
    1. Nonprofit organizations—United States. 2. Nonprofit organizations—Law and
    legislation—United States. I. Entrepreneur Press. II. Title.
    HD2769.2.U6K56 2014
    658.1'148—dc23
                                2013047270

Printed in the United States of America

18 17 16 15 14   10 9 8 7 6 5 4 3 2 1

Contents

▲

Chapter 3
Board of Directors: Choosing the Right
Founding Directors

Chapter 8

Equipping Your Nonprofit: Figuring Out What You Need to Run Your Shop and How to Get It 89

Chapter 9

Development: Raising the Funds You Need. 101

Preface

The essence of a nonprofit organization can be summed up as "serving mission, not profit." Whether your mission is saving puppies, feeding children, preserving history, or the myriad other missions that nonprofits set out to achieve, the ultimate goal is to spend what you bring in—wisely, of course—on the mission.

A nonprofit organization's mission statement is extremely important. While the mission statement in the corporate world became trendy around the time of Stephen Covey's *The 7 Habits of Highly Effective People* and eventually turned into another marketing exercise, a nonprofit organization's mission statement has always and truly been the key to why the organization exists at all.

Don't be duped into thinking that just because you don't need to "make a profit," running a nonprofit is easy! Even if donations come rolling in and you find committed donors interested in supporting your mission, the IRS expects nonprofits to run a very tight ship. There are rules to abide by, bylaws to be written and carefully followed, reports to be created. The Form 990—the nonprofit equivalent of the taxpayer's 1040 tax return form—is long and complex. Financials need to be audited.

Smart Tip

Religious organizations are a whole separate status of nonprofit from other not-for-profit organizations such as social service or cultural ones. This book will not cover starting the religious nonprofit, such as a church, in any way. Be sure to seek out very specific advice if that is your goal.

Taxes and financials are just the beginning. Nonprofit organizations must consider almost every aspect that any for-profit organization does—from human resources to marketing to sales (thought of as "sponsorships" in the nonprofit world, but they're sales, nonetheless) to database management. Throw in some extras like a board of trustees, donor cultivation and stewardship, and other things unique to nonprofits, and it becomes clear how complex nonprofit organizations are.

But all that said, don't be scared away! Nonprofit organizations provide essential services to the world and provide some meaningful work to employees and volunteers.

1

Saving the World
Being True to a Mission

The great majority of nonprofits start because someone is on a mission to help serve a need in their community that isn't being served otherwise. That need could be as seemingly obscure as preserving specimens of old appliances to as obvious as helping people who are lacking financial means get basic necessities. In fact, federal, state, and local governments seem to rely on

Stat Fact
Although the nonprofit sector employs 10.5 million people, making it the third largest industry in the United States, the sector accounts for only 9 percent of U.S. wages and salaries.
—from the Center for Nonprofit Management

the nonprofit sector to extend the assistance available to those in need—from abuse safe houses, to addiction rehabilitation, to feeding hungry children, and definitely to pets in need, a need in every community to which the government does not contribute in almost any way and which is fully addressed by nonprofit animal shelters and rescue organizations.

Other organizations keep the cultural aspect of our society intact. Nonprofit theatre groups, literary organizations, art museums, and historic preservation groups ensure that the history and culture of our society are not only preserved, but continue on.

In turn, for helping fulfill the needs of the greater community, these organizations are given nonprofit status in the eyes of the IRS and are not required to pay taxes on the donations they receive. And donors to the nonprofits are further encouraged to donate, not just to help the needy or preserve cultural artifacts for future generations, but also for the pot-sweetener that these donations are (typically) tax deductible. It ultimately is a win-win-win situation—the nonprofit gets to fulfill its mission without dealing with tax dollars, the donor gets to donate for the advantage of tax benefits, and the government gets help fulfilling its mission of taking care of its citizens.

How Will You Save the World?

What is the mission that is near and dear to you? Nonprofits exist in almost every category imaginable.

Medical

Hospitals represent some of the largest nonprofits in the United States. Not only are they large, but they are very complicated and very expensive, each representing millions of nonprofit dollars. Tufts Medical in Massachusetts, the Cleveland Clinic in Ohio, the Mayo Clinic in Minnesota, and Loma Linda University Medical Center in California are all extremely well-known nonprofit hospitals attracting patients from all over the world. They all have giving programs and receive donations from grateful patients or their families or alumni of the university with which they are affiliated. Many nonprofit medical centers have three-tiered nonprofit programs including educational, medical treatment, and research.

But hospitals are far from the only medical-related nonprofit organizations. Most medical associations like the American Heart Association, the American Diabetes Association, and the Multiple Sclerosis Society are well known to the general public. Nonprofit associations exist for almost any medical condition. Their mission is typically three-fold: to educate patients through workshops, programs, written materials and online information sites; to assist patients with managing their lives with a particular condition or disease; and to donate to, encourage, and otherwise facilitate research to help manage and cure the disease.

Many medical/health-related nonprofits are started because of a personal experience with a particular disease or condition. Some are perhaps not quite as large as the national associations and nonprofit hospitals mentioned above, but are huge nonetheless. The Michael J. Fox Parkinson's Research Foundation bears the name of the famous actor who has publicly shared his diagnosis with the world; the foundation seeks to find a cure for Parkinson's disease. The Susan G. Komen for the Cure, formerly the Susan G. Komen Breast Cancer Foundation, was founded by Komen's sister, Nancy G. Brinker, who promised her sister she would do everything she could to find a cure for the breast cancer that ultimately took Susan's life. (The Susan G. Komen for the Cure organization experienced some negative publicity that will be discussed later in this book as an example of how to—or how not to—deal with bad press resulting from decisions or statements made by an organization.)

Smaller medical nonprofits are also common. In Colorado, the Roundup Fellowship is celebrating the 40th anniversary of its effort to help people with developmental disabilities lead a better life. And the compassionate Balloons for Luv is a 501(c)(3) that provides Mylar balloons with cheerful messages to kids receiving medical treatment for serious illnesses.

Later in the book we will hear from Catherine Poole, founder and executive director of the Melanoma International Foundation, who started the foundation because of her own experience with melanoma and the difficulty she had finding useful information to help her with

Bright Idea

Before starting up a whole new nonprofit, investigate whether your non-profit idea might fit as a branch of an existing nonprofit.

her own battle with the disease. Now 22 years a survivor, she became determined to help other people find information and assistance and started her organization a decade ago.

Education

Perhaps the second largest nonprofit sector is education. The biggest players in the education sector are, of course, the major universities and private colleges. They seek significant support from alumni who graduated from their school and went on to do great things—with fond memories of their alma mater, these graduates often write very large checks to the college/university that helped them be so successful.

Universities, like hospitals, have vast infrastructure. When they want to build a new building or complex devoted to a specific educational topic, they start with a behind-the-scenes search for that huge donor that will be given "naming rights." The Cummings School of Veterinary Medicine at Tufts University, The Anderson School of Management at the University of New Mexico, Rockefeller University in New York, are a few from the endless list of departments and entire schools named after the person who put up the funds to found a school or was a key donor to a specific academic department.

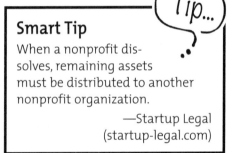

Smart Tip

When a nonprofit dissolves, remaining assets must be distributed to another nonprofit organization.

—Startup Legal
(startup-legal.com)

Sometimes, a department is named after a famous alum or past faculty member to commemorate the person's contribution to the success of the establishment. For example, the Fiske Kimball Art Museum at the University of Virginia was named for the man who was the head of the first art and architecture department at the school.

If your nonprofit startup will have a facility, offering such visible naming rights to significant donors is a great source of funding. We will discuss how to conduct the various stages of such a campaign and some unique ideas for naming opportunities in Chapter 9 on fundraising. Even if you don't have a physical building, don't discount this potential source of funding.

The Arts

One of the things that distinguish us humans from the rest of the animal world is our ability to appreciate something that is considered nonessential to the basics needed for existence—art. (There are many who would argue that the arts are essential to existence, but you get the drift here!) "The arts" encompasses music, fine art, performance art, and literature.

Communities of any size often have an abundance of small and medium-sized theatre troupes. The small "city" of Portsmouth, New Hampshire—whose population has never topped 30,000—is a vibrant waterfront city within easy drive north of Boston and has been home to several regional and local theatres for decades. The community seems determined to care for their art groups through thick and thin.

Larger cities are typically home to anchor nonprofits in each category: a symphony, an art museum, perhaps an opera house, and a large library. Many times these are housed in historic buildings whose preservation through a local nonprofit historic preservation group or a "friends" of the building group becomes a source of community pride—and helps keep the organization alive and thriving.

Museums of all kinds fall under the arts umbrella. There are museums for practically everything you can imagine. Within a 40-mile radius of my rural home is the New Hampshire Farm Museum, Boat Museum, Children's Museum, two small natural history museums (the Woodman Institute and the Libby Museum), and the Wright Museum dedicated to the World War II home front. All nonprofits. And all with a mission to keep alive the history of something that someone—or, often, several someones—felt the need to preserve.

Fine art museums, of course, are key institutions in many larger cities. The Metropolitan Museum of Art in New York, the Art Institute in Chicago, the Getty Museum in Los Angeles are all large, well-endowed institutions. Some are the result of the vision of one person, or a family, to preserve a collection of important artworks or a style of art. Perhaps you have in mind a smaller art museum—everything started small at some point!

Service

Service organizations include social services, but also much more. Perhaps you want to teach people how to build wooden boats or do repairs on their home or write a book. Often these activities are programs offered through a nonprofit with a broader mission. The Loft Literary Center in Minneapolis, for example, offers classes for writers but also holds events and offers resources to writers in their mission of being "dedicated to the advancement of writers, fostering a writing community, and inspiring a passion for literature."

▲

Conservation groups such as local land trusts, and statewide and national organizations, provide a watchdog service of keeping tabs on natural resources and development, particularly in sensitive environments, and land use that is detrimental to a specific species. They do the hard work of holding and monitoring easements that might otherwise not be done, and much more.

Social service agencies help vulnerable and/or low-income populations in a community. Think things like food pantries that provide basic necessities to those in need, free or inexpensive legal services, a safe house for abused women and/or children, support services for the elderly such as Meals on Wheels, or organizations providing transportation for those unable to drive themselves to the grocery store or doctor, or animal shelters that help the community care for homeless pets and help citizens who no longer can care for pets for myriad reasons.

These service nonprofits often supplement or in fact replace local, regional, and state agencies and provide for their citizens.

This is where the nonprofit sector shows how critical it is in providing the most fundamental services to the community. In fact, during periods of economic strife such as that we experienced in the first decade of the 2000s, it is doubly difficult when federal dollars are cut for these kinds of services and people turn to nonprofit organizations for help but donations have slowed for them as well, making it hard to provide services.

The IRS Categories

The Internal Revenue Service, under the 501(c)(3) designation, has its own categorization of nonprofit status. The main type of nonprofits, Type 1 under Section 501(c)(3), includes educational, concerned with public safety, literary, religious, promoting amateur sports, and cruelty prevention of both children and animals. A little light reading to become familiar with IRS publication 557 (see irs.gov/Forms-&-Pubs) before categorizing your nonprofit is not a bad thing to do.

Beyond those general categories, the IRS further delineates nonprofits using such categories as "private foundations" (think of the ones you hear associated with NPR or PBS programming—the Getty Foundation, the John D. and Catherine T. MacArthur

Foundation, etc.) and "public charities," including research groups and educational institutions.

According to Nonprofit Central ("Types of Nonprofits," startnonprofitorganization. com), there is also a "quasi-nonprofit" category, a mix of nonprofit and for-profit which is a very complicated business structure for someone looking to start a nonprofit.

Last, advocacy groups that are formed specifically to influence public policy and government are not considered 501(c)(3) nonprofit organizations under the IRS tax code. If you plan to do any advocacy in your nonprofit, be very careful to investigate the specific laws regarding advocacy, lobbying, and politics. There is some small amount of advocacy work that is allowed a 501(c)(3), but you need to know very specifically for your type of nonprofit organization how you can go about this—perhaps by hiring a separate lobbyist using money designated specifically for that purpose, or perhaps only a certain percentage of your revenue can be used for advocacy work.

Other IRS Startup Information

The IRS online has a fantastic section on its website called The Life Cycle of a Public Charity. The link is: http://irs.gov/Charities-&-Non-Profits/Charitable-Organizations/Life-Cycle-of-a-Public-Charity. This outline covers all the ways that the nonprofit startup will intersect with the IRS; it includes what you need to do every step of the way to make sure you are in compliance with the IRS rules.

The Life Cycle starts with a list of all the organizing documents you will need, from your bylaws, to your EIN application, to your 501(c)(3) determination letter to the Form 990 (covered in detail in Chapter 4 on Finances).

You cannot find a better way to be sure you are following all the appropriate

▲

processes than checking this Life Cycle and following the steps. The IRS online information will be the most up to date you will find, including the ways that you can jeopardize your tax-exempt status.

The Numbers

According to the *Nonprofit Almanac* prepared by the National Center for Charitable Statistics published in 2012 by the Urban Institute, there are more than 1.6 million nonprofit organizations in the U.S. registered with the IRS. 1.6 million. That is a lot of nonprofiting. And that is where you might want to think long and hard about whether you need to add another nonprofit to the list.

The Almanac also goes on to state that almost 60 percent of those organizations are classified as public charities, such as arts and cultural organizations, environmental groups, animal shelters, education, and health-related nonprofits. The good news is that in the decade from 2000 to 2010, the Almanac reports that revenues for these public charities increased by 43 percent; the bad news is that expenses increased by 53 percent.

Almost 50 percent of the revenue stream for most nonprofits categorized as public charities came from fees from providing services and cost of goods such as educational tuition and adoption fees at animal shelters.

Size

While many nonprofits consist of just one or two paid employees and operate on a budget of under $100,000, don't think that just because an organization is nonprofit it has to be small. The Susan G. Komen for the Cure reported $400 million in earnings for the fiscal year ending March 2010—that is not your mom-and-pop nonprofit organization! While few nonprofits will get that large, it is a good example of how the sky's the limit in your vision of your nonprofit.

You should definitely have a vision, and if you envision your organization getting large, that's great. But start manageable—whatever that means for the organization you have in mind and the resources that you have gathered. Like for-profit businesses, nonprofits get large through planning and implementing the plan in a methodical fashion.

Lastly, grow for the right reasons. For-profit companies grow to make more profits—and provide more money to their owners or shareholders. Nonprofits don't grow for growth's sake. A nonprofit grows in order to better fulfill their mission—feed more children, save more homeless pets, preserve more works of art and have a space for the community to enjoy the art the nonprofit is preserving, expose more people to theatre arts, or help starving writers and artists.

The goal of a nonprofit is to use all the revenue brought in to serve the mission for which the nonprofit was established. This thinking is part of the basis for many nonprofits' bylaws, which regulate that when the organization receives a donation of stock, the stock must be sold within two to three days. Donations to the organization are to be used for the sake of the mission; money is rarely used to make money.

Lessons from a Big Nonprofit

The Susan G. Komen for the Cure Foundation, started by the sister of the woman who died of breast cancer for whom the foundation is named, is a huge nonprofit that found itself embroiled in a controversy that brought the foundation down several notches. An announcement in January 2012 set the Komen Foundation down a road of unexpected crisis. According to a report in *The New York Times* in November of 2012, the foundation saw boycotts of not only the foundation itself, but of corporate sponsors as well.

The media attention paid to this move (which was quickly reversed) was equal to the enormous size to which the nonprofit had risen. The lessons, however, are for every size nonprofit. If controversy does find you, face it head on; find a communications consultant to help if you don't have a communications director on staff. And perhaps most importantly, focus on your mission more than ever before. Do as the Komen Foundation did and get back to the stories of real people who your organization is impacting. Unfortunately, the Komen Foundation's blunder, as reported in the *Los Angeles Times* on January 8, 2014, has had long lasting impact with their revenues down from $348 million in 2012 to $270 million in the fiscal year ending in March 2013. Imagine one decision costing your organization 22 percent of its revenue and the reality of how quickly things can change will help any organization focus.

Let's Get Started!

If after reading this chapter you are ready to move on with starting your nonprofit, that's great! The nonprofit sector does amazing work helping the most vulnerable in communities, from hungry children, to abused women, to homeless pets. The sector also makes sure that we continue to value the humanities and the things that make humans distinct from the rest of the animal world—the creation of art, literature, music, and thought-provoking ideas and inventions.

> ## Tip...
>
> ### Smart Tip
> Make sure you are telling the whole story of your nonprofit's service. For example, animal shelters do not provide services just for the furry critters that end up homeless—they provide a critical service dealing with the unwanted pets in a community.

Without the nonprofit sector, a significant piece of the economy in the United States would be lost. While starting a nonprofit is not simple or even easy, the rewards can be enormous. Like starting a small business, start slow and focus on planning. Plan for the launch of your nonprofit and plan for growth and your nonprofit is likely to succeed!

Before Opening Your Door
Setting Your Nonprofit Up for Success

Y ou have your idea. You are convinced that your

idea is best served by being set up as a nonprofit organization, not

as a small business. You've done due diligence that there is not

another nonprofit (or for-profit business) that is accomplishing the

mission you have set for your organization. You have also explored

whether or not there is an organization that is doing similar work or work within your sector that you could establish yourself within using them as a "fiscal sponsor" instead of creating a whole new nonprofit organization (often appropriate for a mission that has a clear end-point, such as helping rebuild after a disaster).

If you have done all this, and still decide your idea and its mission merits its own organization, you are ready to start the process of establishing your nonprofit.

Smart Tip
Do you know someone as committed to your cause as you are? Consider having a co-founder—not only does it spread the work, but it spreads the word exponentially by having that many more connections to contact about your nonprofit.

Checklist for Starting a Nonprofit

- ❑ Identify a need.
- ❑ Research other nonprofits to see if that need is being filled.
- ❑ Research how your nonprofit could fill that need.
- ❑ Decide on a name—make sure it is available through your state's Secretary of State office.
- ❑ Line up a board of directors according to the laws in your state.
- ❑ File articles of incorporation with the appropriate office in your state.
- ❑ Create bylaws.
- ❑ Apply for EIN through IRS.
- ❑ File for 501(c)(3) tax-exempt status using IRS Form 1023: Recognition of Exempt Status Under Section 501(c)(3) of the Internal Revenue Code.
- ❑ File for tax-exempt status in your state, if applicable.

Incorporating

Once you have filed your organization's "articles of incorporation" with your state, your organization is now considered to exist. The articles of incorporation contain the following (in most states):

- Your organization's legal name
- Your organization's address and other contact information
- The purpose, or mission and perhaps vision, of the organization
- The fiscal agent, if there is one
- The names of the board of directors

This is the document that officially designates the creation and existence of your organization, similar to any other business.

Bylaws

Your bylaws is one of the most important documents of your organization. This document outlines everything about the way you do business. Bylaws are the set of rules by which your nonprofit will operate. Bylaws include many details that will come up in other places throughout this book. These details may include but are not exclusive to the following:

- The parameters for selecting a board of directors, including a range of the number of directors, the term of the directors, how directors will be appointed/elected, how the executives of the board will be determined, and any guidelines for how replacements will be made if directors step down before their term is up
- Guidelines on the use of donations such as bequests and gifts of stock
- The curation of artifacts, rules regarding deaccessioning and/or sale of items in a museum's collection
- The hiring of, review of, firing of, and replacement of the executive director
- The rules for changing the bylaws
- Membership rules, if applicable, including whether the organization is required to have an annual membership meeting

▲

Nolo.com recommends putting rules and regulations in the bylaws as much as possible, as opposed to putting them in the articles of incorporation, which are much more complicated to change than the bylaws. Think of bylaws as an operating manual—when things change, you can change the operating manual.

The All-Important 501(c)(3) Tax Status

The IRS tax status known as 501(c)(3) is the key to your nonprofit non-taxed organization. Apply for this as soon as possible; you will use the resulting tax status letter often. Log on to the IRS site at irs.gov and search for Form 1023, Application for Recognition for Exemption Under Section 501(c)(3) of the Internal Revenue Code.

Tax Deductible

Donations to your 501(c)(3) organization are tax deductible by the donors with certain criteria. The responsibility on the organization's part is to document donations and acknowledge them with a formal letter (see Chapter 9 on development/fundraising for further details). Do not give advice to donors, but refer them to a tax accountant or to the IRS publications regarding charitable donations. The IRS is very specific regarding tax deductibility of charitable donations.

Public Charity vs. Private Foundation

When the IRS makes a determination on your nonprofit status, what they have to go on is what you present to them. Nolo.com defines public charities as groups who "derive most of their support from the public or receive most of their revenue from activities related to tax-exempt purposes." They go on to explain that "Most groups want to be classified as a public charity because private foundations are subject to strict operating rules and regulations.

"Under IRS regulations effective September 9, 2008, all new 501(c)(3) groups will automatically be classified as public charities for the first five years as long as they demonstrate in their Form 1023 that they reasonably expect to receive qualifying public support. These rules eliminate the requirement that new groups applying for 501(c)(3) tax-exempt status seek an advance ruling on their public charity status.

"For the first five years, the group will maintain its public charity status regardless of how much public support it actually receives. After the initial five-year period, the IRS will start to monitor whether the group receives the public support necessary to qualify as a public charity."

The Founder's Role

If you are reading this book and planning to start a nonprofit, chances are you are considered the "founder" of the organization. Many times there are several people looking to serve a mission and all would be considered founders of the organization.

If you are the sole founder, you need to decide what you want your role to be as the organization gets underway. Do you plan to serve on the board and be an overseer while hiring an executive director (ED) to run the day-to-day operations? Or do you plan to be the day-to-day person taking on the ED role while you look for community members to fulfill the board of directors? Not surprisingly, there are benefits and drawbacks to either scenario.

The person who thought up the idea to create the nonprofit that will serve the identified need and fulfill a mission is likely the person with the most intimate view of how to best do what needs to be done. In some ways, that person can best serve the organization by being a member of the board of directors, likely the chair or president, offering a big-picture view of the work that needs to be done and how best to accomplish it.

However, that person with the founding idea may in fact be the best person to be the executive director who is going to roll up her sleeves and work tirelessly taking on all the roles that need to be taken on to accomplish the mission. The choice of what role you, the key founder of the organization, choose to take on is often dependent on personality traits and the type of work you like to do. If you are more visionary and not detail-oriented, being chair of the board is perhaps the best fit. But if you are really someone who wants to be a boots-on-the-ground person doing the work of

▲

the mission, then perhaps executive director might be the best role for the founder as the organization gets underway.

Money may be the real deciding factor. Many nonprofits start life as a solely volunteer organization with a working board of directors that divides up all the roles that the nonprofit needs in order to get going. Boards of directors are almost 100 percent of the time an unpaid board, while executive

⚠ **Beware!**
Don't assume that because you are new you won't need to file financials with the IRS at the time of submitting Form 1023 requesting tax-exempt status. You should plan to create pro formas (or estimates) of your profit and loss statements for three to five years.

directors are typically paid positions. Organizations often start with working volunteer boards getting the organization's finances in shape until the point when the financial status of the organization shows that it is ready to pay a director. Or perhaps a grant application is approved that asked for funding for an ED for a specific period of time (typically one to two years) with the idea that the ED would do what needs to be done to improve the organization's financial position to the point of being able to sustain paying the ED on its own.

Board of Directors

Whatever the initial board of directors is doing—oversight only or oversight and worker-bee—along with 501(c)(3) status comes the requirement to have a board of directors. The size of the board of directors is variable. Some states have specific rules regarding size of the board in relation to the size of the organization.

Typically you want enough directors for a good representation of the constituents you serve and the design of your organization. The specifics are covered in the chapter on boards of directors (Chapter 3), but in general if you are a medical organization, you will want a doctor on your board, a museum might want an art curator on the board, etc. Your board will also want to be sure to represent the geography of your organization—if you are a statewide organization, a board member from every county or region is important; if you are a countywide organization, a board member from at least all the significant-sized towns in the county will be useful. Most organizations also benefit from having a lawyer, an accountant, and a banker on the board. Those are the kinds of board development considerations to keep in mind while fulfilling the requirements of the IRS, the state, and your bylaws.

Executive Director

An executive director may or may not be in the cards for your startup organization. Executive directors are the CEOs of nonprofit organizations. They run the day-to-day business, manage employees, and are responsible for income and expenses and keeping within budgets. If the nonprofit has a location, the ED is typically on location.

The executive director reports to the board of directors. The board should plan to review the ED annually, establish goals, and determine whether or not those goals are being met.

Many organizations do not hire an executive director until the organization is operating in the black and has the funding to pay a director's salary. See much more about EDs in the separate chapter (Chapter 5) on this important position within the nonprofit organization.

Lining Up the Right Professionals

You don't need a huge budget to get the help of professionals. But getting the help of professionals is critical—the classic example of how spending some money now will save you money down the road. It helps to find professionals who have nonprofit experience; or, perhaps professionals who do not have nonprofits in their portfolio but would like to add nonprofit clients to expand their reach would give you a great hourly rate to learn with your nonprofit.

Bookkeeper

A bookkeeper is almost essential. Many bookkeepers work for themselves for many clients. They spend a few hours here, a few hours there. Having a bookkeeper come regularly—every Thursday morning, every Monday afternoon, whatever—costs little and saves lots. Your bookkeeper will prepare deposits, pay incoming invoices, prepare outgoing invoices, reconcile bank accounts, keep track of donation pledges and invoices for those that are due, and much more. If you have employees, your bookkeeper will prepare payroll, and keep track of payroll taxes and vacation time. A bookkeeper will keep your financial reports up to date. And they will alert you when something is amiss.

For the small nonprofit, all this really will take only a few hours a week. And it is well worth every penny.

Accountant

An accountant will take your financials to a higher level. They will close out your books at year-end and help you prepare your financials for the auditor (see below). They might prepare your IRS Form 990. An accountant will do a higher level of accounting work than the day-to-day, week-to-week bookkeeping.

Lawyer

Even if you have a lawyer on your board of directors who will do pro bono work for you, it is important to have legal representation at the ready for anything that might require a lawyer who doesn't have a conflict of interest by being on your board. An outside lawyer might also help you see things from a different perspective that someone invested in your organization might not see, especially in the startup phase. A lawyer will help you pinpoint things you need to cover yourself for and help you see things that are potential liabilities that might not cross your mind. They can help with trademarking names, name changes, and most anything legal. Having a lawyer on retainer or at least on standby and familiar with your organization is critical. Just because you are a nonprofit does not mean you can't be sued.

Auditor

An auditor for a nonprofit is someone who comes in and reviews all your financials—from your process to your final reports—and verifies as someone independent of your organization (an "independent audit" is how it is often referred to) that you are doing things legally, above board, and that your books are all in order. An independent audit is not cheap—$10,000 is perhaps a low figure—but many large grants require that you send audited financials, so it is another one of those areas where spending money is important in order to get money.

Marketing

Even nonprofits need to do marketing. A professional may be the best way to get your message out to potential constituents or donors. If you are starting a museum or

> **Beware!**
> Burnout is as real for founders of nonprofit organizations as it is for small business owners. Don't let all your hard work and commitment to your mission go out the window simply because you've exhausted yourself. Find colleagues and learn to delegate!

attraction that you want people to visit, having marketing brochures that can be placed at key tourist sites or in mailings or even at the chamber of commerce is critical.

Nonprofits also advertise, especially if they put on events that need attendees to be successful or have a site that they want people to visit. Marketing professionals can put together the right advertising piece for you.

A marketing professional can help a startup nonprofit with branding—coming up with a logo, an image, a slogan, or whatever that people immediately associate with your organization. Think the Livestrong yellow wristband or the red cross of the American Red Cross Association. These are unmistakable identities.

IT

Chances are your organization will be using computers in some capacity. Whether it's one lonely desktop or a network of laptops, having someone to call on when things go haywire is invaluable. This is the kind of service you line up before you need it—when you need it, you will be desperate to get help. That's not the time to be browsing around looking for someone to fit you in.

Your IT solution does not have to be expensive nor does it have to be a big technological outfit. Many independent, self-employed individuals have made themselves very computer literate and can help a nonprofit with their technological needs and dilemmas.

You might start by finding someone to walk through your plans with you and help you decide what your technological needs are for startup and plans for down the road a year or two out. They might even be the person who will research a donor database that's right for you or, if you do the research yourself, they certainly are the ones who will help you get the database up and running (see more on donor databases in Chapter 9 on development/fundraising). What you don't want is to wait to identify an IT person to help when your system has crashed and you have a donor mailing on its way out the door to meet a deadline and you can't print mailing labels or download a mailing list or whatever you need.

Again, this can be an on-call person, but you want to establish a relationship before you ever need technology services.

Other Professionals

There are many other potential professionals that you might want to hire or have on call. Animal shelters typically have either an on-staff veterinarian (if they are a large, well-established shelter) or, at the very least, a veterinarian whose license they operate under to be able to do certain things themselves in house like vaccinations (especially ones like rabies with legal ramifications) or administering prescription medicines. This kind of relationship is critical for expediency and cost effectiveness.

A museum might want to have a curator at the ready to help with determining if a donation for the collection is worth retaining or better to sell for funds to collect items that the museum would really benefit from having.

In many instances, having established a relationship with a professional is definitely worth doing ahead of ever needing their service. Having one on the books may assure grant funders or other donors that you have the expertise on hand to do what you need to do.

Location

This chapter is titled "Before Opening Your Door." The first real question is, do you need a door? And if so, what kind of space does that door need to open into? It's a rare organization that doesn't need at least an office space, even if it is just one room.

Homebased

Perhaps you have a room in your home that you can use while you get your nonprofit underway. But the home office for a nonprofit brings with it some concerns similar to having a homebased business. Some questions to ask yourself are:

- Is your home office space appropriate for meeting people? These people could be potential funders, major donors, suppliers, board members. You need to be sure your home insurance covers people that are meeting you there for your nonprofit organization's business.

- If the answer to the above is "no," are there other options for meeting people? Perhaps your organization is small enough and casual enough that meeting people at the local coffee shop is acceptable. Meeting in public spaces like this might be okay for some meetings and for some period

Smart Tip

Check with the National Council of Nonprofit Associations (www.council ofnonprofits.org/) to see if there is a nonprofit incubator in your community that can help you get started with low-cost sharing of resources.

of time as you start up, but you won't want to meet major donor prospects in such a public environment. Maybe meeting a prospect for lunch or dinner in a restaurant with a more private area can solve that need. Perhaps your community has a business that rents office/meeting space to people on a short-term basis. Some larger nonprofits allow small nonprofits to "rent" their conference room, sometimes even for free or for a small donation.

- Will you be able to professionally conduct business, whether it is over the phone or via Skype/Facetime, without being interrupted by your young children, your dogs barking at the UPS courier, your parrot screaming (just because that's what parrots do), or your kids playing video games on the other side of the living room from where your office desk is?

- Can you disengage yourself from the housework and yard work around you as you try to work from a home office? Sometimes it is just better to get out of the house and focus on the task at hand without distractions. And often it is best just to separate your home life from your work life, especially if you have a family.

Renting Office Space

Ultimately, professionalism is as important in the nonprofit world as the for-profit world. Potential donors want to give to an organization that looks like it will succeed. However, there is a fine line between looking like you can succeed and looking like you are being excessive—donors don't want to give to wasteful nonprofits, either.

So take it slow on the location decision if you can. You may decide that a one-room office would suffice for quite a while as you get your nonprofit up and running. That doesn't have to mean it has to be in your home. Check around town for whether a bank

▲

or law firm or other business that tends to have a lot of private office spaces might have an empty office that you could rent (or perhaps they would even donate the value of the rent) for a set period of time. Make it at least one year so you don't have to spend all your time scrambling for the next office space.

Many nonprofits operate out of vacant houses in the older districts of small cities. Perhaps they have an empty room in the house that you could use. This can be a win-win where they could fully utilize their space and get some rent income while you can avoid committing to a space until you know what you need or want or until you get large enough to warrant getting exactly what you need.

Other Space Needs

A service nonprofit may have very specific needs, especially if you are providing medical or food services. Look for suitable spaces that are vacant—the building that

---

Agricultural History

The New Hampshire Farm Museum in Milton, New Hampshire, began in the 1970s when some friends started talking about the frustration they felt seeing farm implements rusting and rotting in fields and barnyards across the state. They decided to start preserving some of these tools for posterity and were established under the name the New Hampshire Farm Museum long before they had a space to display them.

In the late '70s, a property was bequeathed to a statewide land trust that included a few hundred acres and a huge, classic connected-building farm structure. With two barns, a shed, and a two-story house, and the knowledge that the land trust would want to focus on the land and not the buildings, the founders of the Farm Museum knew they had found the home for their collection. The land trust was agreeable to them acquiring the building along with some of the acreage. The collectors began the years-long process of bringing their collection home to roost—all in 17 chock-full barns scattered across the state!

The New Hampshire Farm Museum continues to this day with the mission of ensuring that generations to come have a place where they can learn about the long history of agriculture in the state.

---

was full of doctors' offices that have all moved into the new medical high-rise built by the local hospital can make a great medical-related nonprofit location. The longtime restaurant that shut down when the owners retired can serve as a practically ready-made soup kitchen with the appropriate seating and commercial kitchen.

Even if you are a service nonprofit that is going out into the community to provide services and not having the community come to you, chances are you will still need storage space. Food and some medicines may have the need for refrigerated space. Medicines that are delivered with syringes and needles will need locked storage.

Are you starting that toaster museum? Maybe the shuttered Legion Hall would make a perfect setting with open space to display toasters through the decades!

The Next Move

Now that your nonprofit is set in motion, it is time to establish your founding board of directors. You likely have thought of many potential candidates already; many of them may be people you consulted with before making your decision to go ahead.

Board of Directors
Choosing the Right Founding Directors

Starting a nonprofit requires creating a board of directors (also called board of trustees) that oversees the operation of the nonprofit. Members of the board are volunteers like any volunteer for the organization. Selection of a board is a critical aspect of startup.

A mature nonprofit may have a multitude of criteria when looking for potential board members. The startup, however,

Stat Fact

"Almost one-third of chief executives report that they do not have the right board members to effectively govern their organizations."

—2010 BoardSource Nonprofit Governance Index

is going to want a diverse board representing two key characteristics: an entrepreneurial spirit and an abundance of energy. The startup board will likely be more heavily focused on being a "working board"— one that rolls up its sleeves and does the work of the nonprofit to fulfill its mission and help make it a sustainable operation.

Another useful trait of board members who are in on the ground floor is that they have connections in areas that are key to the success of the nonprofit. For example, if a nonprofit is a medical-related organization, having a preponderance of board members that are in the medical industry somehow or another—nurses, doctors, radiologists, medical assistants—will be helpful in having ready access to key information and issues pertinent to the organization. Likewise, if the startup is an animal shelter, having board members that are veterinarians, veterinary technicians, dog groomers, dog trainers, pet food supply store owners, animal control personnel, etc., brings a lot of expertise into the organization on a volunteer basis.

Always useful to a startup nonprofit are board members who own their own small businesses. Starting a nonprofit is not unlike starting a small business. In their tenure at the launch of your nonprofit, these small-business-owner board members will bring experience and knowledge that will help get your organization up and running and poised for growth to the next level. And they may own a business that can be useful in the operation of your nonprofit—board members with small businesses often contribute financially to the organization by offering free or deeply discounted goods and services.

Lastly, it is helpful to have a board member or two who hasn't been in on the evolution of the idea—these are the people who will gently challenge the board as the organization really gets underway.

A Board's Purpose

What is the key function of a board? Ellen Koenig, former Director of Education and Resources of the NH Center for Nonprofits in Concord, New Hampshire, and now a nonprofit consultant explains it like this: Companies (at least publicly held ones) are owned by shareholders. Shareholders get dividends from the company's profits.

A nonprofit is designated with the no-tax status by the IRS in exchange for community benefit—i.e., the taxpayers are agreeing to allow this fundraising organization to not pay taxes on those funds. So essentially the nonprofit is owned by the community (the shareholders) and the board represents the community's interest in the nonprofit seeing that funds are used wisely and in support of the mission.

For these reasons alone it is important that the board pays close attention to finances and insists on complete transparency of the organization.

Executives

Four members of the board are elected as the officers of the board—president, vice president, treasurer, and secretary. In a mature organization, the executives are elected by the entire board; for a startup organization, the founder may serve as the board president or, if the founder is to be the executive director, the founder may pick a board president and together they gather the other three board executives. Then the five of them can work on pulling together board members, the total number of which is directed by state regulations and in the organization's bylaws. Another approach would be to gather a full complement of board members according to the bylaws you have established and let them pick the four executives from the group.

President

The board president, whether in a startup or a mature organization, needs to have strong leadership capabilities. In a startup, the president should be someone with whom the executive director (if there is one at this stage, which will be discussed further on in this chapter) can have a good working relationship since the president and the director will work fairly closely. The board president should be totally committed to the mission of the organization.

▲

The president, especially of a startup organization, should also have deep connections to the community that are most meaningful to the mission of the organization. For example, an advocacy organization that spends a lot of time in the political arena speaking up for their constituents at the state legislature would best have a board president who is politically connected and who can get the attention of the state legislative members and perhaps the media. An organization that relies on events to fundraise will want a board president—and other board members—who are well connected in the business community to garner sponsorship support of their events.

Vice President

The vice president's key role is to sub for the president when he or she is not available—for instance, the VP would facilitate a board meeting at which the president could not be present. For a startup, which needs all the leadership it can get, the VP might also take on a particular project, event, or task as the VP's pet project. And there may also be a key role that the VP can take on—perhaps be in tune with the personnel and provide an HR function, be the lead on reviewing the ED, etc.

When picking the VP, keep in mind that this person is quite often the natural pick to assume the presidency of the organization if the president "terms out" or steps down. The VP certainly may have a different style and a different overriding agenda (that still meets with the mission), but the VP also needs to be in line with the mission. And the VP needs to have leadership capabilities to take on the president role. Just because someone is the vice president does not mean that they have to be made president (unless that succession is mandated in the bylaws).

While it could be awkward if the VP does not assume the top position, the best interests of the organization should always be the top priority. If the VP is not the best choice for the president position but it seems that person expects to be president, the ED will need to begin a behind-the-scenes campaign to talk with other board members about the situation. Everyone should be prepared for the two top positions becoming vacant if the VP leaves if he or she wanted and expected to become president and that isn't in the cards.

Don't always assume that is the case, however. There are many board members who are content with the placeholder VP

Smart Tip
Consider listing your board opportunities on places like boardnetUSA, Bridgespan, or LinkedIn.

Tip...

position and who would support another candidate for the presidential vacancy. If the relationship between the ED and the board, the board president and VP, and among the board itself is strong enough, it may not be surprising that the VP is happy not to assume the presidency. Some people deceive themselves about their leadership capabilities and other people know they do not enjoy the top spot and prefer supportive positions.

This all said, the vice president position by no means should be looked upon as a throwaway position. The best boards have a specific role for the vice president—perhaps the chair of the annual key fundraiser or the person who attends several events representing the organization, or the board member who knows how to write grant proposals. This key role will be unique to your organization; the point is, don't overlook using the VP position to fulfill a key function on the board.

Treasurer

Quite logically, the person chosen as treasurer should be good with numbers. However, the real skill here is not as bookkeeper; the organization should have a day-to-day bookkeeper that records income and expenses and prepares financial statements. The treasurer is more of a big-picture person—the treasurer should be able to read the financials and interpret them in

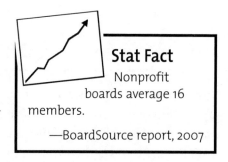

Stat Fact
Nonprofit boards average 16 members.

—BoardSource report, 2007

order to report to the board any anomalies for the reporting period and other specific line items on the financials that the board should know about.

She or he should also be able to answer the board's specific questions about the financials and be able to help the director prepare financially related reports and research. For example, if the organization wants to purchase a donor database, what is the best way to fund such a purchase and what kind of purchase arrangement is best for the organization?

Secretary

A key role of the secretary position is to take notes at meetings and produce minutes. It is helpful to offer the secretary some training in minutes-taking. You want to avoid word-for-word transcription of meetings, but the secretary needs to know to capture the key discussions and decisions of the meeting.

Stat Fact
The 2012 Nonprofit Governance Index reports that 45 percent of non-profit board members are women; Fortune 500 boards of directors, in contrast, are comprised of 17 percent women.

—First Nonprofit Group, "Women are Playing a Bigger Role on Nonprofit Boards" (firstnonprofitcompanies.com)

It may be good to revolve the secretary position on an annual basis. The only drawback to this is if the secretary is a great fit for the executive committee team (made up of the four board officers). But what often happens is that the secretary is so busy writing down the meeting's contents that she or he often has little ability to participate in the meetings.

The Rest of the Board

The remaining board members fill the mandate set by your state (in New Hampshire a nonprofit board must consist of no fewer than five unrelated people) and, subsequently, your bylaws.

Committees

Some boards have a strong committee structure, others do not. It really depends on the kind of organization you have, how large the nonprofit is, and how the board was originally established to function. Committees are a great way to get key, targeted work done. However, be careful not to overwhelm your board with committees—establish only those committees that are essential to the accomplishment of the mission.

Before establishing any committees, think carefully about whether an ongoing committee is necessary or whether a more short-term structure such as a "task force" is more suitable. People are often reluctant to sign up for committees, which seem like they will be comprised of endless meetings, but they like the more temporary structure of a task force. Semantics aside, it really revolves around how you present the group. For example, if the organization needs to hire a new executive director, it is pretty clear that a search committee is short-term—once the new director is hired, the search committee has done its job and is abandoned.

Most organizations of any size have the following standard committees:

- *Executive Committee.* This is comprised of the four executives who carry out policy issues as are often prescribed in the bylaws.

- *Development Committee*. This fundraising-focused committee is usually comprised of a couple of key board members who have experience and/or a propensity for fundraising as well as a couple of community members. These community members are often strong supporters of the organization and are well connected in the arena of the nonprofit's mission. They may not be (or see themselves to be) skilled at fundraising or cultivating new donors (although it is great if they are!), but they can provide useful information in recognizing potential supporters of the organization and helping shepherd them to a meeting that may result in a donation and long-term support. The development committee focuses on fundraising, but that large topic can include discussion about planned giving efforts, membership, major donor cultivation and stewardship, key events—the list is almost endless.

- *Events Committee*. For smaller organizations that do events, a general events committee makes sense. Sometimes, because events typically serve as key fundraisers, the events committee is either absorbed into the development committee or is a subset of that committee. If an organization does substantial events, this committee often has a revolving membership and a different chair—and perhaps entirely different committee—for each key event.

- *Board Development Committee*. This committee can be ad hoc, established when new board members are needed. However, it is never too early to be targeting and developing new board members who may be ready to step in when a board member has to unexpectedly step down, or terms out according to the bylaws. This committee maintains a list of potential board members solicited from the existing board as well as from the community at large. They should be charged with the task of setting up visits to either a board meeting

---

The Life Cycle of a Nonprofit Organization

IDEA → RESEARCH → PLANNING → DETERMINE SPECIFIC MISSION →

GARNER SUPPORT → RETAIN BOARD → IMPLEMENT MISSION → REVIEW

PROGRESS → CONTINUE ON OR DISBAND

▲

or the nonprofit (if it has a site, such as a museum) and creating an initiation plan including the key elements of a new board member packet as well as a tour of the site, if appropriate.

Other committees may be important, depending upon the mission of your organization. If you give out grants, for example, you should be prepared with a decision-making committee that reviews all proposals and either chooses or recommends the top few candidates to the board to choose the final recipient.

Board Packets

Be sure that your board members—those on the inaugural board and those who come on after your organization is up and running—get formal packets of information about what it means to be a board member for your organization. Some of those things should include:

- *Written mission statement, vision statement, and brief history of the organization.* Make it easy for your board members to sound knowledgeable about your nonprofit when they chat it up to other people.

- *Two copies of a "conflict of interest" policy*, one of which should be signed and stored with the organization's important papers. Conflicts of interest generally fall into the realm of hiring a board member's firm to receive compensation from the organization, or even one step removed of hiring a board member's relative to do paid work. It's not that it can't be done, and in fact often is since many organizations rely on the contacts and connections of their board members to supply services at reduced rates, but there are very specific procedures—such as the related board member recusing him- or herself and leaving the room when the vote for such work is taken—that should be clear to everyone in order for all business of the board and the organization to remain transparent. These potential conflicts, and how they are to be handled, are outlined in the conflict of interest policy statement, and how they are handled in fact are recorded in the minutes of the relevant meeting.

- *Your organization's complete bylaws.* These will outline when, where, and how often board meetings take place; a board member's length of term; how many meetings a board member can miss before being replaced. Other non-board-related policies are also outlined in the bylaws; for example, there may be a statement about the rules concerning gifts of stock (most organizations require that gifts of stock be sold within two to three days) or, in the case of a museum, the deaccessioning policy of artifacts in the museum collection.

- *An event schedule for as far ahead as you know it.* While this kind of thing can (or at least, should) be easily accessed on your website, letting new board members know right upfront what upcoming events are on the calendar gives them an immediate chance to arrange their own schedule to attend one or two, but especially key events.

- *Financial expectations.* Board members of most membership-based organizations require all board members to join the organization at some level and to donate to the organization's other key fundraisers. Board members are usually expected to donate at whatever level is comfortable for them. They need to know that grant funders and other donors expect the board to be strong supporters of the organization on whose board they sit. These measures are typically more in the form of "100 percent of our board has donated to the Capital Campaign to renovate the museum," not how much each individual board member contributed.

- *Any other expectations.* Perhaps you want every board member to sit on one committee or pick one major event in which their involvement is required (e.g., "You must attend a minimum of [x number] events and donate a minimum of [y number] dollars each year"). While these are reasonable expectations, don't be so rigid as to scare away potential board members. You want them to use their talents in the very best fit for the organization, not fit into a predetermined mold. Maybe one board member can donate $30,000 a year to the organization but can't possibly attend three events while another barely can meet the minimum membership requirement but has event-planning experience and knows some tricks of the trade that can exponentially multiply the fundraising aspect of a given event. Both have value, and setting too-strict guidelines will limit the number of valuable board members you can find who want to join your organization's board.

> **Smart Tip**
>
> The Nonprofit Resource Center in Sacramento, California, "advises that organizations not have any employees serve on the board so as to not confuse the issues of authority and supervision."

The board packet doesn't need to be extensive but should be complete enough to allow a new or prospective board member to read it through in a sitting and feel pretty confident that she or he knows what is expected of a board member of your organization.

Board Development

The topic of board development can be, and is, a book in and of itself. There are consultants and speakers who make a living from doing presentations and helping organizations with board development (see the Resources section in Appendix B for some of these). Koenig, formerly from the NH Center for Nonprofits sees board development as a critical issue to organizational success—it's important, she says, "to build relationships between board members, getting them to simply like each other. One easy way to do this is to build how are you time into the regular board meeting. Instead of shutting down this casual conversation, encourage it and make time for it. We need to give ourselves more permission to give more time to doing this work." Many people, she says, join boards to meet and interact with other interesting people. They are not going to remain on the board long if that kind of interaction is discouraged.

Simple Workshops

Make sure to alert your board to workshops and seminars happening locally that you think would be of value. Let them decide if they can make it or can afford it, but be sure they at least know about them. One thing these workshops provide is an opportunity to meet and hear from people on the boards of nonprofits—they will get great ideas, learn that other boards/organizations deal with the same things your board does, and learn that other boards deal with much worse!

Consultants

Early in your organization's development, it may be helpful to hire a consultant to do a board development session tailored specifically to your organization—its setup, its stage of development, and the board's experience or lack of experience being board members. Consultants have many skills that they bring to the table, but two key ones are:

- Experience with other boards that they can relate to the team—there is nothing like relating true anecdotes to make clear what works and what doesn't;
- An unbiased perspective—the consultant goes away, cashes your check,

> **Bright Idea**
> Many programs exist to help an organization with board development. The cost of such training should be considered a good use of resources.

and doesn't need to care (although they all do care) whether you succeed in implementing the tips of the session or not.

Board Retreats

Another key vehicle for developing relationships among board members is through board retreats. The members of the board gather at a place and spend some social time together. In national, highly developed organizations, these retreats may be pretty fancy and consist of a weeklong jaunt to Bermuda to hole up at a resort. However, most nonprofits—and certainly those that are startups—can get a significant development experience out of a considerably more modest gathering. It can be as simple as an evening potluck at a board member's house, a weekend gathering at a board member's or other friend to the organization's summer cabin, or one-day excursion together visiting another nonprofit in another part of the region that is similar to yours, and dinner afterward to compare your organization to what you saw that day.

For example, an historic museum's board could visit any type of museum and look specifically at how the other museum's collections are done or what they seem to be able to finance that you have yet to be able to do. Or a zoo board could visit other live animal zoos or animal-focused organizations. Don't be afraid to arrange to have the director or board member of the organization you are visiting speak to your group, especially if you are not in direct competition. Organizations love to compare notes about how other groups fundraise, deal with membership, balance programming with events, manage volunteers, etc.

Executive Director Review

One key role of the board of directors of any organization is to oversee the executive director, including an annual review. This is the kind of human resource

▲

development that nonprofits should definitely take a page from the for-profit world and implement. According to BoardSource's Nonprofit Governance Index 2012, "an annual performance review is central to the Executive Director's satisfaction."

This task is typically taken on by the executive committee. The committee should meet in advance especially to discuss what goals they feel the director should strive for in the coming year, particularly as they pertain to the current strategic plan. The president or VP then could take on the task of creating a work plan for the upcoming year to accomplish the goals set out for the director. This is a place to discuss salary, whether the director has met goals for a raise this year, and what the director needs to accomplish in the coming year to get a raise at the next review.

More discussion of this review comes in Chapter 6 on employees. Suffice it to say here that the executive director reports to the board, particularly the executives of the board; the board should treat the executive director like an employee and allow him or her the respect of any employee/employer relationship.

Executive Session

The closed meeting format of "executive session" allows the board of an organization to discuss privately any sensitive issues that would benefit from the ability of board members to feel more free to engage in robust discourse. These sessions should be occasional and should be on topics that protect and advance the best interests of the organization. According to the Board Source document, "Executive Sessions: How to Use Them Regularly and Wisely" (read the full document by registering as a guest at boardsource.org or search the document name and find other locations who have posted it, such as unitedwaync. org), executive sessions are most often used for personnel issues, executive performance, or peer-to-peer board discussions. The document further explains that "as a governing body, the board needs to demonstrate and exercise its independence from the chief executive. For example, a nonprofit board serves as a check-and-balance when accepting the financial audit and determining chief executive compensation." It further cites succession planning as another topic for which executive session is important.

Board Liability

According to *Get Ready, Get Set*, a publication by the California Management Assistance Partnership created to help nonprofits get solidly off the ground, "under California law, directors bear all legal authority and responsibility for governing a nonprofit organization . . . . Careful attention to the legal standard of care will help board members avoid liability."

Every state has different laws covering liability risks for board members of a nonprofit. You should check the laws in your state during the planning phase of your nonprofit startup and be prepared to let all potential board members know not only their responsibilities but also their liabilities.

All nonprofits should carry directors' and officers' liability insurance ("D & O"). The cost of such coverage varies, but the organization should plan to carry this coverage. Bodily harm, nonbodily injury lawsuits, and claims of mismanagement of assets are the typical claims that board members might find themselves subject to. However, there have been instances of board members suing other board members or employees suing board members for things like wrongful termination, discrimination, or sexual harassment.

Get Ready, Get Set points out that "D & O policies vary greatly . . . . When shopping for a policy, there are three major items to keep foremost in mind: Who is covered and who is not; what types of lawsuits are excluded from coverage; and what is the rating and payment history of the underwriter."

In many states, the board is not held liable for anything but assuring that the payment of workers' compensation taxes are up to date. Whatever your state has for a policy, however, does not mean that you cannot be sued and be subject to the cost of hiring a lawyer. Board liability insurance seems fundamental.

Youth Board

One of the biggest complaints heard from nonprofits is the concern about

---

Bright Idea

Consider developing a "youth board." Or, at least, create a youth position on your general board. Having youth involved in oversight provides organizations—especially those with a naturally older constituency—with a younger generation's perspective and provides an organization with potential future full board members.

Smart Tip

Tip...

"The Sarbanes-Oxley Act was originally passed to strengthen corporate governance, but has had a strong, if indirect, impact on nonprofit governance," says the Urban Institute. Many nonprofits, UI found, have voluntarily adopted some provisions such as external audits and a written conflict of interest policy.

engaging young people. This complaint comes from all corners, such as the ability to engage young volunteers to the ability of an organization to reach young volunteers. Much of the discussion revolves around the organization's use of social media—considered the key tool for communicating with the young generation.

One way to connect with youth is to engage them on your board. High school students especially are looking for ways to enhance their appeal to their college picks—active volunteerism and knowledge in the study area of their choice is definitely a way to do that.

Youth boards do not need to be as large as your regular board. Getting them involved in a specific area—managing the details of your key annual 5K fundraiser, for example—is an angle to take where you get them fired up on a specific task. And they have the knowledge to utilize all the appropriate ways to engage youth.

All-Volunteer Organizations

Some nonprofit organizations, especially startups, do not have any paid staff at all. The board performs all the duties, responsibilities, and work of the organization required to fulfill the mission. This can work for a long time, maybe forever, depending on the work and mission of the nonprofit.

Many times this is a way to get a startup organization up and running; when the organization gets a little more mature and has met an established goal of success in fundraising, it then starts to hire key paid positions. Often the first paid staff member is an executive director. Or, a lower-level position is hired with the intention of eventually making this person the executive director when the organization is ready to fund this key staff position and the individual has proven him or herself a good candidate to run the nonprofit.

When an all-volunteer organization reaches the stage of hiring a director, the board does not jump ship altogether. The board of such an organization will continue to be very much a working board, but it will need to prepare carefully for moving from doing the work to directing the work. This period is critical, and executive directors, says Ellen Koenig, often do not survive the transition. The organization—perhaps before hiring a director or in conjunction with the new director, or more likely both—should map out a very specific transition plan for the

> **Fun Fact**
>
> A common saying regarding board members is "Give, Get, or Get Off." Crude perhaps, but it points directly to how important the function of fundraising is when it comes to a nonprofit board.

gradual relinquishing of duties by the board. Or, more appropriate, a gradual move of the board from certain work to other kinds of work.

Perhaps the new director's strengths are in programming. Move the board away from day-to-day programming tasks and into more behind-the-scenes work, like cultivating new corporate donors. Or the new director is a fantastic fundraiser—from grant writing to major event planning—and the best role of the board becomes organizing programs and reaching out to local experts to present programs at the organization's site.

In general, the board should envision stepping back and letting the new ED create a community identity around his or her leadership. The eventual goal is for the board to really step into an oversight, behind-the-scenes role, and away from a day-to-day operations role. It is critical, says Koenig, "to find meaningful work for board members after the transition."

Fundraising

This chapter would be remiss if it didn't emphasize the importance of the role of fundraising for any high-functioning board of directors. Besides their job of governance of the organization, every board member should take on fundraising as a prime responsibility of their participation as a board member of the organization. Every board member can also take this responsibility on in the way that suits them the best—meeting with potential major donors, encouraging the business community to contribute, or coordinating a key fundraising event. Let the board member choose their method, but boards should not be allowed to forget this key role.

▲

Board Power

Hopefully this chapter has made clear the enormously important role the board of directors has in not only the success but in fulfilling the legal obligations of any nonprofit organization. Choosing board members carefully and with the mission and needs of the organization in mind is critical. Don't consider board development to be frivolous—in fact, it is essential.

A Founder's Advice

The Melanoma International Foundation (MIF) was founded in 2003 "to provide the scientifically sound guidance and support our founder could not find when she was diagnosed with melanoma." With a mission to "develop personalized strategies with patients so they may live longer, better lives" and a vision of "a future where top-notch melanoma treatment is accessible to all patients globally." A key goal is early detection through education. Founder Catherine Poole offers the following advice to those starting a nonprofit:

- ○ Be certain that you really want to keep at this after the organization is launched.

- ○ Keep in mind that running a nonprofit organization is basically the same as running a business.

- ○ With the above in mind, be sure not to look at it all from your heart.

- ○ Even if you run the organization for a long time by yourself, as she did, you will eventually need to deal with having to hire others.

- ○ As editorial director, you should run the board, it shouldn't run you.

- ○ Staying small may work best for your organization.

- ○ Find ways to keep connected with the people your organization serves in order to stay motivated.

- ○ Be sure to create a succession plan so that the organization you worked so hard to create keeps going when you give up the helm.

4

Finances
Numbers Count, Even for a Nonprofit

If you are thinking of starting a nonprofit because you don't like dealing with financial statements and other money matters, you are going to be disappointed. The directors, managers, and board of a nonprofit need to be as financially astute as any for-profit business—perhaps even more. Nonprofit organizations may not pay taxes and may not be designed to make a profit, but don't for a minute think that income and finances are not important! Anyone who starts a nonprofit organization and is happily thinking they aren't going to spend a lot of time on financial statements is in for a big surprise.

All of the spreadsheet players of the for-profit corporation apply to the nonprofit—and even a few additional. And that includes startup pro formas and budgets. The P&L, balance sheet, IRS Form 990, and budget worksheets should all become familiar to the key managers of any nonprofit organization.

Financial Professionals

Your startup phase is the place to bring in the financial managers who will be part of your organization. An accountant well-versed in nonprofits is well worth the cost, as is a bookkeeper, at least part time, right from the get-go.

Bookkeeper

A bookkeeper will take care of the day-to-day accounting for your nonprofit. This includes calculating and generating paychecks as well as making sure payroll taxes are paid and the IRS is kept happy with all the regular employee taxes and considerations. Your bookkeeper will also prepare bank deposits, pay invoices, and keep your checking account balanced.

Using accounting software such as QuickBooks, your bookkeeper should be able to get you financial information when you need it—or the ED should be able to look in QuickBooks and pull needed information as well, especially if your bookkeeper is part time.

Accountant

Your accountant will do the big end-of-year tallying and reconciling of all your financial information, much of which will be provided by the bookkeeper. The accountant will prepare the all-important Form 990 (more on this in a minute). And the accountant might be your key liaison if you have your financials audited.

Financials for the Business Plan

Like any for-profit business, you want to start your organization's financial life with a business plan that includes "pro forma" (or speculative) financials, especially an income-and-expense statement, better known in the for-profit world as a profit and loss statement, or P&L. Since nonprofits do not exist to make a profit, a more accurate term for this financial statement is an income-and-expense statement.

A detailed income-and-expense statement is typically done for the first year. The next three to five years are less detailed, showing only the larger categories of income and expenses, such as "programs" in general rather than a list of each program you plan to offer and what kind of income you expect from each.

If you are starting your nonprofit with commitments (known in the nonprofit world as "pledges") or actual donations already in hand, perhaps a building either donated or purchased for the use of your nonprofit which it will own, and some equipment, you should plan to include a balance sheet that shows your assets.

Some of this is speculation, but your speculation should be well informed by research and discussions with nonprofit managers in a category similar to yours.

While many nonprofits—including many successful ones—have been started with little or none of the above, but simply a gut instinct by a person or group of people

> **Tip...**
>
> **Smart Tip**
> Keep in mind that getting grant money from almost any source is a slow process. If you think grant money is a strong potential source of seed money for your organization's startup, you will want to start that process at least a year before you plan to open your doors.

and has been grown organically, from the ground up, it is still best to have some sort of business plan in hand to not only show to potential donors/investors, but also to use as a guide.

SWOT Analysis

A common business tool is the SWOT analysis. SWOT stands for Strengths, Weaknesses, Opportunities, and Threats. The SWOT analysis is useful for the nonprofit organization as well. You can use this exercise as a great way to think through

▲

the startup of your organization and as a great tool for working on a three- to five-year strategic plan.

These categories cover the following:

- *Strengths.* What makes your nonprofit different from others? This includes you and your personal experience, but it also includes any special distinction about your mission and any unique way you plan to deliver on your mission.

- *Weaknesses.* What will make your mission hard to accomplish? Does your "business plan" rely on income from event sponsorships but your organization is located in a rural area where there are few businesses that might sponsor your events? Or there are a few businesses but there are already several other unrelated nonprofits that those businesses are sponsoring? Will your mission delivery rely on transportation and highly fluctuating, expensive fuel costs that leave you with an inability to accurately estimate your costs?

- *Opportunities.* Is there another nonprofit with whom you might collaborate, whether it is in delivery of service or simple sharing office space? Can your museum space accommodate a small museum within the museum? Or perhaps offer classroom space to a nonprofit offering workshops?

- *Threats.* For example, does the aforementioned fluctuation in fuel costs make it impossible to predict your income needs?

Brainstorm at least a couple of things in each category that apply to your idea.

Startup Funds

You will need your business plan, your SWOT analysis, and your income and expense analysis at least for the first three years in order to start approaching sources of startup funds. If you have a strong category that might lend itself to seed money from grant funders and foundations, it's worth subscribing at least for a month or two to a couple of the grant databases such as the Foundation Directory (fconline. foundationcenter.org) and do an intensive search for potential grant sources for your nonprofit.

A quicker way to get funding than to count on grant money is to research people with means who might have a personal interest in your mission and approach them for seed money. This is completely different from the for-profit business looking for an investor who would be interested in getting a return on their investment. This type of backer is not getting investment return in the form of money but in the form of believing in your mission and seeing it happen—and, of course, if you are a 501(c)(3), this investment can be a tax deduction.

The Form 990

IRS Form 990 is the 1040 form of the nonprofit world. The 990 is only required by the IRS if revenues for your organization reach over $50,000 a year. However, it will

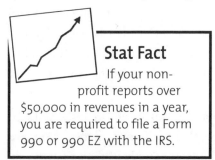

Stat Fact
If your non-profit reports over $50,000 in revenues in a year, you are required to file a Form 990 or 990 EZ with the IRS.

typically be required by most grant funders to submit your 990 with any grant application. It is a public document that, if you are listed on nonprofit sites like GuideStar, is available for viewing by anyone with a computer anytime.

Applicants for employment can look on your 990 to see how viable your organization is. Potential funders can review it to see where your money is going. A nonprofit should never have anything to hide; having a publicly viewable 990 should not be a problem.

Financial Independence

If you are the founder of your startup nonprofit or in on the ground floor in any capacity, be sure to keep your personal finances completely separate from the organization. Open a separate checking account from the first time you receive or expend money.

The upshot is, treat your nonprofit professionally. Don't mix up little expenses here and there. Document donations, even those that are in-kind such as computers or office furniture, and document expenditures from $15 to send a grant application via overnight mail to $1,500 for the first month and security deposit of a lease on office space.

Debt

If you can avoid debt, do. That said, having a line of credit established with a local bank is helpful when you need to solve a problem or jump on an opportunity.

One common way that nonprofits use debt is to secure a loan against pledges. Pledges are commitments of donations payable over time. So someone might pledge $10,000 to your organization, payable over five years at $2,000 per year. Perhaps you have numerous pledges that have been committed in order to complete the renovation of your facility, allowing you to increase the number of constituents that you serve by as much as 50 percent—perhaps with renovations to the existing soup kitchen that your organization runs, you can serve 150 people per meal rather than 100. In your campaign to raise money to do these renovations, 25 people have in total pledged over $100,000.

You should be able to go to a bank that has already shown itself to be friendly to your organization and its cause (they have sponsored an event or held some kind of event themselves in support of your organization) and obtain a loan for $100,000 to essentially bridge the gap between the time you will have received the commitments of these donations to the time you actually receive the funds.

Before you do this, however, be sure you have formally ensured all of these pledges. Donors should sign and date pledge forms that outline the pledge they have committed to, the time frame in which they plan to complete their pledge payments, and specification of how much they plan to pay on their pledge in what time frame.

These written commitments 1) should be entered into your donor database and the donors sent pledge invoices at the appropriate intervals and 2) the written and signed pledges can be gathered and shown to a bank as proof of commitment—and you should set up your repayment plan to reflect the amount you will get in pledges at the time the payment is due.

Do not forget to send follow-up invoices to pledge donors. In the case of those who forget to send their pledged donation in the specified time, make sure the person who has been assigned to the donor follows up in person to let the donor know how important the timely payment of their pledge is to the organization and its ability to accomplish its mission and make timely payments of any bridge loans.

Budgets

Like with a for-profit business, budgets are critical for the nonprofit to succeed. The budget process for your startup phase should be relatively simple. It may not be simple to create since you are guessing about a lot, but it should be a relatively simple budget. The budget will show the expenses that you will incur to accomplish the mission and goals for, say, your first year in operation—if it is way too complicated, that may be a good sign you are biting off more than you can chew for your first year out. After you have a budget in place, you can then attach numbers to the income you need to generate in order to cover these expenses (see page 48 for a sample budget).

The Small Numbers

When it comes to budgeting, try to think of everything. Salaries and rent or mortgage are easy to put in there. But getting down to the nitty gritty can take a little more thought and perhaps some research. While printer ink is not a huge line item like the rent, it certainly can add up pretty fast at $60 to $75 a pop. You may not need to figure it out down to the calculation of how many pages per cartridge your printer's ink will do and tally out how many pages you think you will print in a year. But if you think you will use one ink cartridge change per month and you have two printers in the office, that is close to a $1500 line on your annual budget, which makes printer ink a significant budget item.

Donations

Account for everything you will need—office supplies, paper towels and toilet paper for the bathroom (especially if your nonprofit is a public space like a museum with public bathrooms!), desk chairs, supplies for program-related activities, a refrigerator for the snack room.

When you get to the income side and how you are going to budget the purchase of these items, you can start to figure out what kinds of things can be donated and accounted for as "in-kind" donations. So even if you don't end up having to purchase items you still have accounted for them. Don't omit things just because you can "probably get that donated."

Ultimately what all this means is that your financials need to represent a clear picture of your organization—both to you and to anyone who would like to see them.

Petty Cash

Petty cash is a small but important necessity in most organizations. Employees that need to run to the post office or the office supply store or the craft store to buy a last-minute item to finish a project or mail a grant application should not need

Sample Budget

The Appliance Museum FY 20xx

Income		
	Grants	$25,000.00
Grants		**$25,000.00**
	Admission fees	$25,000.00
	Workshop fees	$ 5,000.00
	Retail store	$35,000.00
Earned income		**$65,000.00**
	Direct-mail appeals	$12,000.00
	Memberships	$ 6,000.00
	Appliance day event	$ 8,000.00
	Sponsorships	$ 5,000.00
	Online donations	$ 2,000.00
Fundraising		**$33,000.00**
Total Income		**$123,000.00**
Expenses		
	Payroll related	$ 6,000.00
	Insurance	$ 5,000.00
	Staff salary	$64,500.00
	Fundraising expenses	$ 4,500.00
	Marketing, printing	$ 8,000.00
	Admin costs	$ 6,000.00
	Professional fees, misc.	$ 4,000.00
	Facilities	$25,000.00
Total Expenses		**$123,000.00**

to spend their own money to do so. If they want to purchase these things and get reimbursed, that's fine, too—it's a little more paperwork, but it still keeps close track of expenditures. Petty cash can make it easier, but be sure to keep track of petty cash expenditures, too.

The Board Treasurer

The board was covered in detail in Chapter 3, but when it comes to the organization's day-to-day financial life, where does the board treasurer fit in? Really, the board treasurer fits in everywhere, but the key role of the board treasurer is not in the nitty gritty—that is, he or she does not need to be involved in the decision to purchase office supplies. But if the office supplies expense line is looking unusually high for the past couple months, the board treasurer will point that out in the review of the monthly finances.

The board treasurer can help you see the financial big picture that can be influenced by the details.

Audit

Many grant funders ask to see audited financials. Accounting firm EisnerAmper (eisneramper.com) offers the following great definitions of a financial audit versus a review:

"A nonprofit audit is an opinion backed by evidence." An audit might confirm that an organization is reporting their pledges correctly based on a review of the pledge recording system used by an organization.

"A review is a report that states that the financials are free from material misstatement." A review looks over the financials and the backup for the numbers and confirms that the financials are accurately reporting the numbers.

> **Tip...**
>
> **Smart Tip**
>
> An audit is expensive, but even if it is not required for external reasons (e.g., grant funding, especially federal grants), having audited financials "meets objectives of accountability and transparency."
>
> —EisnerAmper, Accountants and Advisors, eisneramper.com

Some state laws even require a nonprofit audit during some defined period. Audits are expensive—an audit of even the smallest organization's financials can cost well over $10,000. They also provide a return, allowing you to apply for certain grants that require audited financials.

Also check with your state's nonprofit association for the possibility of funding available for help with audits for organizations under a certain size.

The Bottom Line

The bottom line about nonprofit finances is that the bottom line is not the only important thing about your finances. Be sure you are being accurate and detailed in the financial life of your nonprofit. It will help you in every possible way.

5

The Executive Director
The Nonprofit CEO's Role in the Organization

The executive director (ED) of a nonprofit organization is equivalent to the CEO of a for-profit company. The title is lately sometimes being replaced with the more for-profit sounding title president or CEO, which eliminates the word *director* and any potential confusion with the board of directors.

▲

The ED runs the day-to-day work of the nonprofit. EDs of startup nonprofits will likely have very little paid staff. The chief job of the ED is to do what needs to be done to fulfill the organization's mission. As the organization grows, this will mean less and less detail work and more and more big-picture work. But for the startup of an organization that chooses to hire an ED right off the bat, the job is both big picture and small details.

Founder as ED

Before getting into the executive director hiring process, the first thing to consider is whether it makes sense for the founder of the organization to be the first ED. This is often the case.

The logic here is that the founder will have a key role in the newly formed nonprofit, so why not have that role be as the ED? The founder probably has the clearest vision of the organization and can set the ball rolling for the future.

In this instance, the founding board likely will be a very hard-working board. But the other dynamic it sets up that the founder needs to consider is that the director reports to the board—so as director, the founder suddenly finds herself in the position of answering to a group of people, which sometimes means defending choices that are clear to the ED as founder, but not so clear to the board as a group.

So, if you are the founder of a startup nonprofit, you might carefully consider being the president of the board of directors and hiring an outside ED. Let's consider that option.

> **Tip...**
>
> ## Smart Tip
> Don't rely on a search only in the nonprofit world for your organization's executive director. Candidates from the for-profit world can bring very useful skills and experience and can learn about nonprofit idiosyncrasies.

Hiring an ED

Hiring an executive director for a nonprofit organization should be done in the same way any hiring process takes place. Before beginning the search, the founder (who could also be the board president) and board members should put together a

The Square Peg Foundation

The Square Peg Foundation is a California-based therapeutic riding program that uses rescued horses for the program, combining working with disabled individuals with animal rescue, two very prominent nonprofit service-type missions.

"2004 was a good time for starting this," says Joell Dunlap, founder and now executive director, "and Silicon Valley loves a new idea/startup."

Eager to build a new model from the best of each—therapeutic riding and horse rescue—Dunlap recognized that the organization was going to need a board of directors that trusted her and were okay with a few mistakes.

The first board treasurer was a nonprofit professional. He told them, "You do the horses, let me take care of the financial end of things." This is just what they needed. But four years in, the treasurer died—and they were devastated.

"We grew because we had to, and I had some fabulous mentors," says Dunlap, including Ann Murray of the Global Fund for Women, of whom Dunlap speaks highly. But it was difficult needing to retool the organization after losing their treasurer, who had the nonprofit knowledge, without the advantage of being a sexy new startup.

"This experience," says Dunlap, "made me into a real executive director. Before I was just someone with a good idea who wanted to beat the odds and improve the model. I don't recommend doing it this way, but it has been a neat thing for me."

She goes on to explain that her interests and experience have evolved. Learning to delegate—often a hard concept for founders and executive directors—has been especially rewarding for Dunlap.

"It took me a lot of years, lots of confidence, to hand the horse part over to the other handlers and volunteers. You need to develop trust. A couple [of] bad experiences, a couple volunteers quit—you can lose that trust really fast. I needed to outgrow that phase in order for the organization to grow." Dunlap explains not only did she learn to delegate, she learned to enjoy delegating. "I find lots of satisfaction in watching people deliver services." One of the things she did to help herself accept delegation more readily was to develop training programs that enabled her to be confident literally handing the reins over to others.

And it all must work—ten years and three locations later, Square Peg Foundation is going strong. "It's always going to be complicated," says Dunlap. She advises "be on the balls of your feet all the time."

▲

job description. This can be done by all members of the board, depending on the way the board is put together, or a separate committee can be constructed specifically for the hiring process. The committee could whittle the field down to the top two or three candidates and the rest of the board or the executive committee could come in at that point and join the final decision-making process.

As mentioned, the starting place for hiring an executive director is to put together a job description. This is important whether a recruiter is doing the search or not (see page 76 for a short list of recruiters). This will enable an ad to be put together that accurately reflects the kind of person you are looking for.

The board should decide what you can afford to pay the new ED. If the pay is low, which it certainly might be with a startup nonprofit, be prepared with some non-monetary incentives—extra vacation time and flexible work hours are all very nice, but if the job is so massive that the ED can hardly fit in a vacation, let alone extra time off, then perhaps those are not reasonable incentives. Consider other flexibilities like working from home part of the time if that could fit the organization. At the very least, be sure the ED has as nice an office as you can manage that is equipped with a decent computer and phone system. Perhaps the organization can pay for the ED's cell phone and other things that are directly related to the job that might help save them some personal money. Be creative so you can attract the best people, even if you don't have the best money to pay them. Burnout comes fast and easy for overworked executive directors, so giving them the best tools you can (and a nice office, up-to-date computer, and company cell phone are still part of the organization even if the ED leaves) can up the chances they will be satisfied for a while.

It can be best to be upfront about the pay in either the ad itself or in phone interviews

The ED Job Description

As for any job, be specific (and honest) about the roles that the executive director will need to fill. They are many and varied. There is no reason to hide how hard the work will be or the known difficulties (no staff, little money). The new director will find out soon enough—and if you are lucky enough to hire an experienced ED, he or she already knows that there is lots of work, little staff, and low pay. It is hard work for everyone involved (including the new employee) to hire a director who gets there without knowing the full scope of the job. Having your first executive director leave soon after arriving does not say good things about the health of your organization. People seeking employment in the non-profit sector must be fully aware of the hard work, little pay, lack of support staff, and that you always have more to do than can be done in a day. They also don't want to be bored!

with the first round of candidates. Let's face it, even though the nonprofit world has a large share of people who consider doing the work of the mission more important than money, people work to earn a living to pay their expenses. Don't waste your time interviewing and getting excited about a candidate who would not be interested in a salary as low as the one you are offering. It is best for all if you at least know you are both in the same ballpark before you get too far into the process.

ED Job Basics

The key responsibility of the executive director of any type of organization is to ensure that its mission is being carried out. The second responsibility is to ensure the financial stability of the organization. These two responsibilities are almost interchangeable, since if the organization isn't financially stable then there is no ability to accomplish the mission.

Beyond that fundamental premise, the basics of almost any executive director job for any organization include:

- Supervising any paid employees, whether they are part time or full time
- With the executive committee's (or full board, depending on the dynamic of the organization) help, setting an income and expense budget

- Fundraising, fundraising, and more fundraising
- Ensuring the maintenance and functioning of any buildings
- Coordinating volunteers if there is not a paid staff member (or a volunteer!) who does that
- Coordinate volunteer recognition events
- And more fundraising!

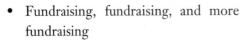

Beware!

If you find the need to have an acting director, do not let the title go on indefinitely—it gives the wrong impression about your organization.

Some executive directors will have the following additional responsibilities, depending on the type of organization:

- Creating a schedule of events for the organization, if events are something the nonprofit does
- Cultivating and stewarding major donors and potential donors, ensuring they stay apprised of what's going on in the organization (this also falls to the board and in some organizations is the board's key responsibility)
- Lining up volunteers for tasks for which there isn't paid staff
- If the organization does not have a development staff member of any kind, keeping the donor database up to date, including sending acknowledgment letters for donations

ED as Chief Fundraiser

If it hasn't been said yet in this book, now might be a good time: All members of a nonprofit organization are fundraisers. Some more directly than others, but all staff and board even by merely being a representative of the organization are giving impressions all the time to potential donors, making them consider whether they want to donate to the organization or not. If you are an animal shelter, the staff at the front desk of the shelter who people first see when they come to look into adopting a homeless pet are shaping those potential adopters' (and often future donors) thoughts about how welcome they felt. And they tell others. Staff conducting field trips or giving presentations to employees at large companies or delivering meals to seniors—any kind of community interaction with staff members (and volunteers) is a key fundraising activity.

But the executive director is the fundraiser in chief. Beyond the board president or any other individual member of the board, the ED represents the organization to the world. And he or she knows the inner workings of the organization like no other person associated with the nonprofit.

> **Beware!**
> Executive directors, especially of startup nonprofits, need to learn how to delegate and not feel like they are the only ones that can do everything. While high energy is key to startup success, the ED who does it all is on the fast track to burnout!

You would do your organization's future a world of good if you made sure to hire an executive director who understands that while there are lots of small fires that can (and sometimes will) suck up a lot of time, the ED must understand and know how to pull away from those fires and remember to concentrate a large amount of time and energy on where the funding will come from for the organization to not only operate but to fulfill its mission. One of the principal ways for the ED not to get overly involved in every small fire is having the ability to delegate to others. (And having others to delegate to!)

Fundraising is the ED's key role and this is best made clear from the beginning. If the person you are interviewing does not seem to understand or know how to do that—which you should be able to find out from asking pertinent questions and calling references—then that person should be crossed off the list of top candidates no matter how slim the list is getting.

Roles and Responsibilities

The ED's role in a startup will depend greatly on how long the organization has operated without an ED. If your nonprofit is new and you plan to hire an ED right off the bat (which is great if you can!), then the ED's role will include a lot of launch-type activities, from getting computer systems up and running, working with a website designer, and perhaps hiring other employees, or, at the least, recruiting the appropriate volunteers for the jobs at hand.

The founder and the board will need to be looking for a very entrepreneurial person to take the helm of a startup nonprofit as their first ED, someone who is capable of initiating many processes, creating departments, and taking on many roles that an ED of a mature organization would not have to do. The entrepreneurial thinker will love this but can be hard to find in the nonprofit world, since entrepreneurship often lends itself to money-making.

That said, many nonprofit leaders fully understand the nonprofit's innovative role in solving a problem. You just need to be sure to be looking for that instinct and drive to create something new from nothing.

Your success in finding such a person will have a lot to do with how much you have to offer. Yes, salary will be important, but nonprofit leaders tend to get as much out of the potential accomplishments of the organization as the paycheck they get for moving things forward.

Stat Fact

In the decade between 2000 and 2010, the number of people employed in for-profit business went down by 6 percent, in government went up by 8 percent, and the number of people employed in nonprofits went up by 29 percent.

—*The Nonprofit Almanac 2012*, Urban Institute Press

Traits of a Good ED

Here is a list of the top five traits to look for as you search for your executive director:

1. *Fundraising capability.* Look for evidence in resumes that the applicant has had success in fundraising. It doesn't have to be just one kind of fundraising; a lot of that depends on your organization. Event planning, grant writing, major donor cultivation/stewardship, direct-mail or phone-a-thon appeals—these are all types of fundraising. Many organizations do them all. But even those that do them all tend to have a focus on one or two of these avenues for getting donations.

2. *Financial savvy.* Your executive director does not have to be from the nonprofit world. Lots of capable people in the for-profit world look to escape the corporate scene and apply to nonprofits looking for a chance to work for a mission, not for a profit. These people often come with lots of experience in reading financials, creating budgets and managing expenses, and reporting financials to their supervisors. The thing to be careful with here is reminding the ED hired from the for-profit world that the mission and money are a fine balance in the nonprofit sector; the balance will tip back and forth between the two, but mission is king.

Traits of a Good ED, continued

3. *Big-picture thinking.* While the board can take up the slack in the big picture of the organization, no one is more intimately involved in all aspects
   of the organization than the executive director. This can be a help and a
   hindrance to big-picture thinking. In a nonprofit where there is not much,
   if any, support staff, the executive director can easily get caught up in the
   details. But knowing these details can also lend a unique perspective on
   the big picture that no one else has. It may be wiser to look for someone
   whose background tips heavily on the big-picture side—it's easy to get
   caught up in the details even if the details aren't the typical strength of the
   person.

4. *Good communication.* The executive director is the key voice of the organization, especially at the startup phase. When an organization gets to
   the size of the American Diabetes Association or the Getty Museum, the
   ED still needs to be a good communicator, but the organization's voice is
   probably going to be relayed through a communications director. In the
   meantime, the chief fundraiser will need excellent communication skills
   and will need to have the ability to switch gears with those skills to be able
   to use the most effective means for different constituents, be it staff or
   potential donors or volunteers.

5. *Delegation.* Look for someone in the executive director position who is
   comfortable with delegating tasks to others. Hand-in-hand with delegation skills are communication skills—unsuccessful delegation often comes
   with not being able to communicate the task effectively enough for someone else to accomplish what was asked of them. An effective communica-
   tor/delegator knows how to be straightforward without being offensive.
   Many people, especially the high-functioning type that tends toward nonprofit ED work, have had bad experiences delegating tasks and tend not to.
   Ask an applicant to describe her or his attitude toward delegation.

There are many, many other traits to look for in a strong executive director candidate—and many traits specific to the way a particular organization
works—but if you look for the five above, you will cover a lot of other ground at
the same time, from how well the person multitasks to how well they supervise
employees.

And finally, on this topic, be sure if you find just the right entrepreneurial spirit that the founder and the board are capable of letting that person use some of that innovativeness. If you want someone to simply implement a plan that is already in place, you don't need someone with the same kind of entrepreneurial drive—in fact, they (and you) will only be frustrated.

In a very large nonprofit, the ED—like the for-profit CEO—will spend a large percentage of any given week managing employees. Even with organizations who have small numbers of employees—all "worker bees" and no managers, for example—the ED will be the one to motivate the overworked employee, manage crises, and mitigate disgruntled employees' complaints.

The ED Relationship to the Board

The executive director reports to the president (or chair) of the board of directors, and through that person, to the entire board. The ED is, basically, a nonvoting member of the board of directors and should not only attend but typically does considerable preparation for board meetings.

The ED and the board president should be in regular contact. The ED should feel perfectly comfortable going to the board president with any concern or problem, whether it's with an employee issue or an emergency with a building or (and perhaps especially) with financial concerns. The president—under the guidance of the bylaws—can decide how much the rest of the board needs to be involved.

More typically, it is *when* the rest of the board should be apprised of a problem, not if. There should be no secrets between the board president and the rest of the board. The board members overall need to feel that they are aware of the organization on whose board they sit and not hear something out in the community that they should have learned about at a board meeting or through an email in between board meetings.

Succession Plan

The executive director is arguably the most critical position at your organization. Having thought about who would step into this position if the current director left or you had to let him or her go is important. If you are the founder but not the ED, you

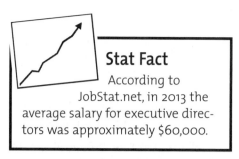

Stat Fact

According to JobStat.net, in 2013 the average salary for executive directors was approximately $60,000.

are probably the likely choice to keep the day-to-day operation of your organization going for some short period of time. But you likely have plenty of things on your plate already, so you won't want this to last for long.

A succession plan typically will target an on-staff person who can take on the role of acting director. If this person is someone that the board thinks would make a good ED and that person would like the job, the acting role gives that person time to prove him- or herself up to the task. Be sure to outline this from the start—don't let the "acting" description go on indefinitely. Give a specified time period in which it is understood that the candidate will either step into the ED role or the board will begin interviewing other potential candidates.

Even if you don't come up with an easy succession solution, you will be glad you have thought about what would happen in the event that the director leaves the position.

Day in the Life of an Executive Director

The following is a view of a day in the life of an executive director. It is a fictional view of the director of a small ($200,000 budget range) nonprofit with perhaps one part-time staff member. The nonprofit resides in a small house which it bought, and an attached building, which it had built, and is a museum showcasing the history of household appliances.

8:30 A.M.: At computer checking and answering emails. One is from a major appliance manufacturer responding to the ED's request for sponsorship of a new exhibit the director would like to put up at the museum, another from an appliance repair person saying yes to doing a workshop on appliance repair, another from the waste pickup company talking about the upcoming increase in their fees, one from a former colleague asking if the director is planning to attend a seminar the next day on social media being given by the state nonprofit association.

9:15: Work on finishing a grant proposal due in overnight mail by day's end.

9:55: Hears part-time museum clerk's car pull in.

10:10: Museum clerk stops in her office to tell her that the machine that does the video introduction for visitors is not working. ED fixes machine, and as she is leaving, visitors engage her in a 20-minute conversation about their interest in the museum. She gives them her business card, thanks them for visiting, and retrieves a copy of the hot-off-the-press newsletter out of an unopened box that has membership and other donation information as well as news about the museum and appliances in general and upcoming workshops. On her way back to her desk, she cleans the office bathroom and removes office trash.

11:30: Back at her computer working on the grant proposal.

12:15: Board member arrives. They are going together to meet a prospective donor for lunch. On their way back, board member suggests they stop in office supply store and she will buy the organization a new wireless printer.

2:00: Museum clerk wants to review the order for the shop inventory she has put together. ED looks at it briefly and asks if she can review it overnight and talk more about it in the morning.

2:20: Back at the computer to wrap up final details of grant proposal. Looks at email and sees that the large appliance manufacturer has replied and said yes to a significant sponsorship of the new exhibit. Can't spend time being excited yet, has to finish grant proposal.

3:00: Finishes grant proposal. Starts making the requisite number of copies when copier runs out of toner. Replaces toner cartridge, gets almost finished with copying when paper runs out. Doesn't have any extra. Runs down the street to a good friend of the museum's and asks if he has a hundred sheets or so of paper she can borrow. He does. She finishes copying.

4:00: Museum clerk is leaving and stops by ED's office to remind her that she is on vacation for the next week and a half. ED thanks her, tells her to have a great time on vacation. ED remembers that tomorrow is her own birthday but she has to work the museum clerk position since that was the only day she couldn't find anyone to come in for the clerk going on vacation.

4:45: Dashes off a quick thank-you note to the prospect they visited for lunch, which she puts in the post box on her way to the overnight courier office with the grant proposal; she doesn't lock up for the day because she thinks they close at 5 so she just leaves. They close at 6. Her grant proposal gets in overnight mail and her thank-you note is mailed, but she still has to go back to museum to close up before going home.

5:20: Back at office, checks email one last time, which includes a reminder that a school group is coming tomorrow for a tour. Grabs some leftover cheese from the refrigerator from an event that previous weekend to snack on while she searches her computer files for that timeline sheet that she always hands out to the group, prints out 30 copies, and makes 30 more on the photocopier using what is left of the paper she borrowed.

6:30: Finally sets the security alarm and heads home, bringing a few folders of information about other possible grants and companies to solicit sponsorship from.

There are many things this ED does to help manage her multitasking day, and there are many things she could do better to help ease the burden of having so many responsibilities. But ultimately, this is often the day of an ED of a small nonprofit, especially a startup—some of it involves the stuff for which you got into this to begin with, some of it involves janitorial work.

Owning a building often brings with it unexpected emergencies and is a constant maintenance task for the ED if the organization doesn't have the funds to hire a building maintenance person or contract with a property manager. These are the kind of behind-the-scenes things you need to consider when you are trying to decide between owning or leasing if you need physical space beyond a simple office or two.

The Face of the Organization

As you can see from this chapter, the executive director of a nonprofit organization juggles many balls. This person quickly becomes the face of the organization. If you, the founder, will not be in the role of ED, it is essential that you find the best possible person to fill that critical job.

6

Staff
The Fine Balance of Having Enough Staff

At the startup phase, as with any small business, do not overburden yourself—both from a financial and from a management standpoint—with staff. Conversely, do not let a slow start get you into the common mind-set of much of the nonprofit world—that staff is considered a bad use of donors' gifts and that everyone should be overworked and underpaid in nonprofit organizations. This mind-set is a perfect recipe for burnout, where you lose great people (including yourself, the ED, or founder of the organization). This means having to retrain people, which is more expensive than paying staff well to do skilled work, supporting them with administrative help, and having them stay with the organization for a long time.

Often the reasoning for lack of support is the misinterpretation that donors do not want their money to be spent on staff; that donors understand that there needs to be a leader but they want their money to be spent on the organization's mission. But it is a rare organization that doesn't require people to accomplish its mission. And if you can provide measurables that show that your approach *is* serving the mission—feeding hungry children, saving homeless pets, or providing a cultural resource—it is the rare donor who will complain about your staff.

Smart Tip

If substances are used in your work environment that are especially harmful if sprayed in the eye, you may be required to have an eye wash station.

All that said, going slow with hiring, especially at the startup phase, is recommended. Hiring a couple of staff members within perhaps a year's time is probably necessary. Of course, a lot of this depends on what type of nonprofit organization you start. A service organization or an advocacy group that does not have, or need, a physical location might be able to accomplish their goals for a while with volunteers who support their cause. But an arts venue—playhouse or museum—that has a long list of functions, from creating marketing brochures to taking tickets to directing plays or curating an exhibit, may find it necessary to have a couple of paid staff right upfront. Volunteers are heroes and the lifeblood of most nonprofits; but there is also something about not being paid that can make people slightly less committed and/or reliable—not what you want when you are just about to open the doors to the public for a big opening.

Of course, you also need to budget and raise money to support whatever staff you feel you need at this stage. When there isn't a staff member doing a necessary job, it probably falls to you. Doing everything there is to do and working 20 hours a day six days a week to do it will result in burnout. Your cause is not helped by you being too exhausted to care or too sick to perform the tasks needed to accomplish the organization's mission.

The Logistics

In order to hire anyone, your organization needs the proper employment logistics in place. Employees are employees, whether they work for a nonprofit or a for-profit organization. Being a nonprofit does not preclude you from being required to follow employment laws and practices. If the ED of the startup organization is paid, then everything an organization needs to hire employees has likely all been put in motion. Let's look at the basics.

EIN

Apply for an EIN (Employer Identification Number, the "Social Security Number" of the business), which you will need for everything from applying for a grant to paying any taxes related to your business. To get an EIN, you simply go to the IRS site (irs. gov) and search the Forms and Publications section for EIN Form SS-4. There is a link to the form itself and to instructions on filling out the form. You can apply online, by phone, by fax, or by mail. If you apply online or by phone, you will get your EIN immediately. By fax or mail can take up to four to six weeks to get your number returned, so plan accordingly.

Workers' Compensation

"Workers' comp" is insurance coverage provided by the employer for workplace injuries. It is required by law and is a top priority on your list when you decide to hire employees. Workers' compensation does not take the place of health insurance, nor does the fact that an employer provides employees with health insurance mean the employer doesn't need workers' compensation coverage.

Workers' compensation is one area where it makes no difference if you are a for-profit or nonprofit organization. All organizations that hire employees are required to carry workers' compensation coverage.

You would obtain coverage for workers' compensation from an insurance carrier approved to underwrite workers' compensation policies in your state. Compliance is under both state and federal laws. While anyone starting a nonprofit organization (or any business) should be aware of the importance of complying with workers' compensation coverage, you don't need to know every detail of this complicated law—a legitimate insurance carrier will know all the laws, right down to providing the appropriate posters that are legally required to post in your workplace.

OSHA

The Occupational Safety and Hazards Administration was created through the 1970 Occupational Safety and Health Act. OSHA's sole mission, according to the website allaboutosha.com that breaks OSHA information down into understandable pieces, is to reduce workplace illnesses, injuries, and deaths. And it has worked—since 1970, workplace deaths, says the site, have been cut by 60 percent and job-related illness and injury has been reduced by 40 percent. You can complain all you want about the details of complying with OSHA safety standards, but the proof is in the numbers.

OSHA doesn't care if you are a for-profit or nonprofit. If you hire employees, you need to be abiding by the OSHA standards for workplace safety. This covers everything from having slip-proof footing in dangerous work areas to making sure the building you work in is up to local, state, and national codes covering egress in case of fire; electrical wiring standards; use of ladders, pallet jacks, and other equipment; as well as hazardous substances.

> **Tip...**
>
> **Smart Tip**
> Directors of any nonprofit organization should be vigilant ensuring workers' compensation payments are always up to date—not only is it the right thing to do by employees, but in most states it is one area where directors are liable whether you have directors liability coverage or not.

MSDS

Materials Safety Data Sheets (MSDS) are available on virtually every hazardous substance that might be found in any workplace. MSDS notebooks are required by OSHA to be available in an accessible place and include sheets on all hazardous substances used in your workplace. The sheets tell what the substance is, what the hazards are, and how to treat an inappropriate exposure.

Other Workplace Concerns

Once you start having employees in your nonprofit, you need to take the laws and regulations surrounding employees seriously. Those concerns include ensuring antidiscrimination laws are followed. Be sure your nonprofit office environment includes a no-tolerance policy for sexist, racist, or ageist language, for example. Don't let this kind of thing get started and you never have to worry about shutting it down once your staff gets larger.

Smart Tip

Tip...

Do not run out and hire someone the minute a new need is discovered. Build up the tasks that the individual could be responsible for and hire when you know you have sustainable work (that results in income or directly serves the mission—or creates time for someone else whose key work results in income or serving the mission) for that position.

Postings

Create a visible place in a common area where all employees will see workplace safety posters required to be displayed by law. When updated information is received, send out a memo to all employees alerting them to this fact. There is nothing to hide when it comes to employee safety and information about antidiscrimination practices. This is the law and it is surely how you want to operate, so being open about it should not be a problem.

Job Descriptions

Any organization that has staff should have job descriptions for every position. The job description is helpful to clarify positions where roles could be overlapping; it provides clarity to each staff member in developing their workload and priorities; it is very useful in the hiring process; and it is even more helpful in the annual review process.

Be clear in the job description about what you want the person in this position to focus on. Don't throw in everything and the kitchen sink—that just looks amateur, like you really don't know what the job is you are hiring for or what that person's priorities should be. It is hard to critique someone's job performance when you have not clearly outlined what the person should be doing.

Beware!

Remember, a nonprofit raises money in order to use it to accomplish the stated mission of the organization. It does not raise money for the sake of having money.

▲

Smart Staffing

The staff hired should either generate income for the organization, accomplish key components of the mission, or do administrative work so that you and other staff members can spend time generating income and/or accomplishing the mission.

Receptionist

If your organization gets phone calls or has in-person visitors, you definitely should have a receptionist. This can be a part-time person who is there during the key busiest hours of your day, perhaps a parent with school-aged children would fit in well with a 9 to 3 workday or a college student looking for a part-time job in the evenings; whatever works best for you. For certain nonprofits this person is the face of your organization; the last thing you want is for someone to attempt to call you several times and not get through. Having a receptionist on staff for your key business hours is an inexpensive way to put a professional face on your organization.

Pick someone who is organized, gregarious, has a cheerful voice, and seems to like people. Be sure to give this person some responsibilities—opening mail, stuffing and sealing acknowledgment letters, keeping track of volunteer hours, even updating the Facebook page or website with information given to her by a key staff member—that occur regularly to make sure she is busy and feels connected to the organization.

Also make sure this person is kept informed so that she is armed with correct information (or what you would like her to say) when asked about things that are going on regarding your nonprofit.

Administrative Assistant

Nonprofit organizations have a habit of considering administrative staff to be a waste of donor money, and that donors would not approve of their donations being used to hire assistants, and that administrative help is fluff. As the saying goes, nothing could be further from the truth.

The first thing you should be clear on is that the administrative assistant is not the receptionist. Although serving as receptionist can be part of an administrative assistant's job, the receptionist is typically tethered to a desk much of the time and has the key task of greeting people, whether it is on the phone or in person.

Often nonprofits are manager and director heavy. Part of what's going on there is that titles are cheap; if you can't pay a high salary, you can give the person an important title. Don't fall into this trap. While you should definitely give the title appropriate to the job and the level of expertise and experience you want in that position, don't give a title thinking it's part of the compensation package.

Instead, consider hiring select people as directors and/or managers, or hire consultants with expertise to help with specific initiatives and then have enough administrative staff that can work under the direction of your key personnel to perform the work that needs to be done to implement the initiatives.

In other words, don't hire people as managers and directors and then have them do administrative work. You are throwing money away if you do.

Volunteer Coordinator

If your startup organization is going to rely heavily on volunteers—either during the startup phase or even after the organization matures—a volunteer coordinator is critical. Volunteers want lots of hands-on interaction with the organization's staff. And it will quickly become apparent that volunteer coordination is a lot of detailed work that can get away from you very quickly.

Another thing about volunteers is that you need to keep careful records of their hours, and have each volunteer log every time they volunteer for the organization. If their work is off-site, the volunteer coordinator will need to track them down each week and get the hours from them to log in.

Communications Manager

Communications in any organization is a big job—it is also a critical job; someone needs to organize communication to the outside world. You should let people know when something great has happened; keep your donors updated on specific things you have requested donations for; and let sponsors, potential sponsors, and the people those sponsors want to impress know that the event they supported was a smashing success.

The other role the communications manager plays is when something goes wrong and you want to get your own message out there before someone else does and gets it wrong. You need someone in the communications role who is ready to pounce on clarifying bad press or deciding not to respond at all.

The communications manager is also in charge of your communications tools like newsletters and your social media posts.

Development Staff

Any nonprofit organization needs one person devoted to development (fundraising) work. What level that person is at depends a lot on who else in the organization is focused on development, to what degree, and what type of development. If your nonprofit will do lots of fundraising events, having a key development person who is essentially an event planner makes sense. A development assistant could then be doing database input and updating, preparing large mailings, and keeping up with acknowledgment letters while the administrative assistant is helping with some of that as well as preparing the incoming checks for deposit and data input.

If events are a secondary or less significant part of the organization's way of generating income, then a development manager or director could be in charge of the key development work—soliciting sponsorships, supporting the board with major donor information, etc.—and the administrative assistant helps with the other details as mentioned above.

Your development staff can be pulled together based on the organization's needs and way of operating. Some specific projects can be accomplished by hiring consultants and contracting work as needed. But the organization should have a key development person who knows the organization's needs and database, and other major parts of how the organization raises money to achieve its mission.

Building Manager

If you have a facility, it is helpful to have someone in charge of managing it. For an organization with one small building, this is likely to be a luxury that can't be justified. However, if you have a complex facility or multiple buildings—especially if they are located miles from each other—having a building manager who takes care of all the issues that can come up can be a huge time saver for the ED and other staff members. Lining up snow plowing, mowing, and repairs is in the hands of this one person—who also takes care of figuring out what to do when these people don't show up. Getting someone on staff who is handy and can fix a toilet, repair a loose stair, or do other things that need immediate attention without having to call out and wait for someone to show up to do it can be a huge relief.

Other Staff

Depending on the mission and activity the organization is engaged in, it may have many other possible staffing needs. Land conservation groups may need specialists in developing easements; theatre groups may need creative staff such as set designers and literary managers; legal assistance nonprofits certainly need a lawyer or two on staff; child welfare groups may need a nutritionist or a psychologist to achieve their mission; many animal shelters have an on-staff veterinarian; museums of any kind will need a curator in their midst.

Beware!
Designate someone on staff—the ED, the bookkeeper, the communications manager—to be the point HR person for your organization. Or hire someone on contract to lead this important function once you start to hire staff.

The list of possibilities is endless. Don't be afraid to hire who you need as long as you budget how you are going to raise the funds for those salaries. But start off slow and remember that it is easier to hire when the need is great than it is to lay off when you realize you just can't support the position.

Compensation

Compensation refers to salary but it also refers to everything else that is part of employees' reimbursement for spending their time using their expertise to the organization's advantage.

Salary

The first thing you will need to consider when setting salaries/hourly rates for employees is what the minimum wage laws are in your state. And then, with that as a baseline, figure out what you can afford to pay based on your organization's budget, then what the market in your area likely requires to competitively get and retain employees in the type of employment you are hiring in. When budgeting, do not forget the employer's portion of Social Security and Medicare which totals 15.2 percent of the employee's salary—the employer pays half that and the other half comes out of the employee's paycheck, which the employer pays on the employee's behalf.

Insurance

Whether your organization needs to offer insurance to workers, only you can decide. Some of the decision-making factors include budget but also how competitive you need to be to get and retain skilled employees.

Health

There was a time when health insurance was firmly connected to employment. That connection has loosened considerably. Now there are all sorts of configurations for health insurance for workers.

Whether you offer health insurance to employees is something you need to decide. Even if the organization does not pay for health insurance, there is savings in numbers; you can offer insurance through a group plan that the employee pays in full but gets at a very good rate based on the number of people in the group.

Life

Life insurance policies are not very expensive and can come as part of an overall insurance package available after a certain period of employment.

Other

Dental insurance can be an inexpensive employee benefit. And pet insurance has become a popular offering, with group discounts available for larger staff.

Vacation

Vacation leave is a simple and inexpensive benefit to offer employees. Most nonprofit jobs are such that if an employee is going to be out for a week, she gets caught up with all timely work before leaving, leaves a couple of tasks to an administrative assistant to move along while she is gone, and then catches up when she returns. Most nonprofit jobs are not of the type that you will need to hire someone to take on the person's job while she is on vacation. So be generous with vacation time, while making it clear that all vacation needs to be coordinated with the ED or the person's direct supervisor.

Sick Leave

A week's worth of sick leave covers most personal sick leave needs. Employees with children tend to take sick leave for themselves and their children too, so think about whether a couple of extra sick leave days might make the difference between hiring someone who happens to have kids. People shouldn't be penalized for having kids— but also make sure you are being equitable to those people who do not have children.

Other Leave

Some organizations offer a couple of days of so-called "personal leave" which can be used when neither sick nor vacation fit the bill. These couple of floater days can also be handy for those holidays, like Thanksgiving, that fall in the midst of the work week but you don't give the day after as vacation.

Retirement

While most nonprofit organizations are not going to offer a formal retirement plan that the organization pays for, it makes good sense to have some kind of company retirement plan that employees can buy into. Instead of the 401(k), the nonprofit retirement plan is the 403(b). It works basically the same—the employees invest tax-deferred money typically from payroll deduction into their 403(b) accounts. At some point in the maturation of your nonprofit, you may get to the point where the organization can provide some modest level of 403(b) match; that is unlikely to be possible right out of the box. But don't ignore creating a retirement investment plan for your employees.

Volunteer Time

Employers can offer a couple of hours each month that an employee might do volunteer work for another nonprofit of their choosing.

Discounts

Joining organizations like the chamber of commerce, or providing employees with a library card or discounts at local companies can be nice perks.

The Upshot of Hiring

To put it all in a nutshell, a barebones budget may point to a bare-bones staff—if you don't have the funding for payroll, you can't hire the people. But building slowly with carefully chosen key staff can actually add to your ability to accomplish your mission and to bring in the funding you need to both support your mission and pay staff. There is no question that it's a fine balance, but "staff" and "hiring" should not be dirty words!

▲

A Short List of Nonprofit Recruiters

Here's a partial list of some of the nonprofit recruiters.

○ Commongood Careers, 38 Chauncey Street #1001, Boston, MA 02111, (617) 542-1404, cg careers.org

○ DRG, 130 East 40th St, Suite 800, New York, NY 10016, (212) 983-1600, drgnyc. org

○ Korin Ferry, 200 West St., 4th Floor, Waltham, MA 02451, (866) 652-9975, korinferry.com

○ Leadership Recruiters, 2200 Arch Street, Philadelphia, PA 19103, (215) 665-1479, leadrecruit.com

○ m/oppenheim Associates, 221 Main Street, San Francisco, CA 94105, moppenheim.com

○ The Moran Company, LLC, 8927 Sagamore Rd, Leawood, KS 66206, (913) 766-1952

○ Opportunity Knocks, 100 Peachtree Street, NW, Suite 1500, Atlanta, GA 30303, (678) 916-3070, opportunityknocks.org

○ Scion Nonprofit Staffing, 576 Sacramento St, 2nd Floor, San Francisco, CA 94111, (415) 392-7500; 319 SW Washington St, Ste 902, Portland, OR 97204, (503) 345-0103, scionnonprofitstaffing.com

○ Third Sector New England, 89 South Street #700, Boston, MA 02111, (617) 523-6565, tsne.org

Volunteers
Heroes of the
Nonprofit Community

For most nonprofits, volunteers are the lifeblood of the organization. And for many nonprofits, volunteer coordination ends up a nightmare. It doesn't have to be this way. But organizing volunteers takes a lot of coordination.

The Volunteer

People volunteer for myriad reasons. Some want to contribute to the cause of the organization they choose to volunteer with. Many retirees volunteer to get out of the house and feel like they are still being a productive member of society. Some people volunteer to socialize with a like-minded community of people. Some simply volunteer because they have gotten themselves in a bit of trouble and need to put in community service hours.

Whatever the reason, Americans are ready, willing, and able to volunteer their time. And your organization should be ready and willing to utilize them.

A Program

The first thing you want to do in order to utilize volunteers is to have something for them to do! Of course, you don't want to artificially create a program just to use volunteers. But sit down with the staff member in your organization who manages program delivery and write down all the possible ways volunteers could be utilized in each program. You'll want to keep this list reasonable; if it gets long, see if you can organize the lists into groups of tasks that one volunteer could perform.

For instance, if your program involves an event, can one volunteer be at the registration booth and once registration is over, can that same volunteer then move on to setting up the snack table in one of the break-out rooms?

Applications

Once you know what you can use volunteers for, you can start the process of collecting names. You will need to collect a lot more applications than you need volunteers. Applicants for volunteer work have great intentions but many dwindle away without ever volunteering or after a couple of times. Life circumstances change, people move, they get new jobs, have children, etc.; the volunteer pool can be constantly in motion.

And, yes, you definitely need an application. First, this can help identify someone's level of commitment and weed out people who are not that interested. If someone is willing to fill out a one- or two-page application, they are expressing a certain level of interest.

Much like an application for a job, an application also formalizes the volunteering process. The potential volunteer is writing down their personal information as well as writing answers to questions like what kind of volunteer experience they have already, any special skills they have that they would like to utilize as a volunteer, and, of course, personal and emergency contact information.

Applications of all volunteers who do end up working in the organization or are still interested but have not yet been called into service should be stored in an active file, which should be weeded out at least once a year, removing any applications for those who have not yet actively volunteered and are no longer available or interested.

Interviews

Plan to do personal interviews with volunteer applicants. First, this shows potential volunteers that you take them and the work they will do for your organization seriously. Secondly, it will provide you with lots of clues as to the commitment level of the applicant as well as other information about them that will help decide what types of volunteer jobs you might want to match them up with—for instance, whether they are outgoing enough to represent your organization to the public or so shy that work behind the scenes might be your best choice.

Stat Fact

In 2012, the average value per hour of volunteer time was $22.14. The per-hour value varies state to state, with 2011 figures showing New York highest at $28.73 and Mississippi lowest at $15.78.

—"Independent Sector's Value of Volunteer Time," IndependentSector.org

Volunteer Orientation

After your in-person interviews, the next step for potential volunteers should be an orientation session. This can be as a group. Set these orientations to happen regularly, perhaps once a month or every three weeks. You don't want them so often that people constantly don't show up since they can always catch one in a couple of weeks.

If you want to use the orientation sessions as another step to weed out volunteers who aren't really that serious, set up a window of time from personal interview to orientation that they must go to an orientation. Do require people to sign up for orientation sessions so you can plan refreshments and make sure you have an appropriate venue for the number of people.

What you do in the orientation gatherings depends a lot on what your organization is using volunteers for. Perhaps you have two orientations a month, each focusing on different types of volunteer opportunities.

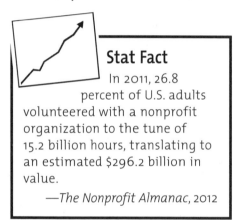

Stat Fact

In 2011, 26.8 percent of U.S. adults volunteered with a nonprofit organization to the tune of 15.2 billion hours, translating to an estimated $296.2 billion in value.

—*The Nonprofit Almanac*, 2012

This can be where you have volunteers fill out release forms or other specific forms depending on what you plan to have people do. Plan to spend time telling the group about the organization and any news or future plans you might like to share that your volunteers will likely get asked about if they are out in the community.

Volunteer Tracking Software

You might have the software or database to track volunteer time right in front of you but haven't realized it. Many donor databases designed specifically for nonprofit donor management have built-in volunteer management software—often it is an add-on to the basic database, and requires an additional fee.

Some volunteer tracking software is online-based and allows you to set volunteers up to input their own hours, saving lots of time if you have a large and active volunteer pool.

Coyote Communications keeps a list of volunteer management software at coyotecommunications.com/tech/volmanage.html. This list is very specific to volunteer management and, although at the time of this writing was last updated in July 2012, the categories it covers for each software is a great list for any software you wish to examine. Things like what operating system is required to use the software and if more than one person can access the software at once are things you might not even have thought to find out about a volunteer management system.

A few of the software companies mentioned are CERVIS (Community Event Registration and Volunteer Management System), DonorPro, GiftWorks Volunteers, and Tapestry. Keep in mind that donor software companies are bought, sold, and absorbed all the time. Contact a few noncompeting organizations similar to yours but outside your area of influence and ask about the volunteer software they use. And ask volunteers if they have used any software at other organizations for whom they volunteer and the pros and cons they experienced using it.

The Value of Tracking Volunteer Time

In an article titled "Tracking Volunteer Time to Boost Your Bottom Line: A Complete Accounting Guide" by Denise Walsh in *Blue Avocado*—a non-profit-focused magazine claiming to provide "practical, provocative, and fun food-for-thought for nonprofits"—gives the following five reasons you should take the time to track volunteer hours:

1. It recognizes that volunteer time is important, which shows volunteers you appreciate them.

2. It is essential in securing funding by showing funders and donors the resources you already have.

3. It proves to funders and donors that you have the people you need to perform your mission.

4. It can help meet requirements for matching funds.

5. A volunteer log can help protect the volunteers themselves and the non-profit in liability cases.

Volunteer Appreciation

Volunteers do like to be thanked. Of course, you will thank them personally each time you interact with them when they are volunteering. But there are many other levels of appreciation as well.

Membership

If you are a membership-based organization, one simple way to thank volunteers is to offer them automatic membership in your organization. This is especially appreciated if membership comes with benefits like discounts at stores that they might be interested in.

Years/Hours of Service

Set up a formal record of hours of service each year. Think about giving an annual recognition of some kind (a certificate? pin? a gift certificate?) to those with anniversary years of volunteerism—perhaps one-year, five-year, and ten-year pins. You might also recognize the person with the highest number of volunteer hours over the past year or you might consider giving something to everyone who meets a certain amount of hours in a one-year period—what that number is will vary depending on your organization and the amount of volunteers you use.

Appreciation Event

Volunteers typically love being part of a community. Having an event where they can socialize with all staff and with each other is very meaningful. This does not have to be an expensive or complicated event. Have it at your site if you have one; if not, find a simple place or one that people love to go to and hold it there. Be sure to pick a downtime for your organization so you are not adding this to a stressful time of the year when lots of other things are going on.

Beware!

If your organization works with youth or other "vulnerable" populations, it is a good idea to require background checks on volunteers.

—"Legal Considerations When Engaging Volunteers," charitylawyerblog.com

Your Volunteers Day-to-Day

People often volunteer with the expectation, and interest in, interacting with staff and other volunteers throughout their volunteer service. This doesn't mean there aren't some people who would love to be given a list of names and be set up at a desk in a corner making phone calls or entering data into a database. But for the most part, people volunteer for the social aspect of it as much as the social service aspect. If you want to retain volunteers, you should recognize that and be sure your volunteer positions are fulfilling that part of the volunteer experience wherever possible.

Keeping Busy

Volunteers do not come to your organization to sit around and wait for something to do. If people make the time and take the effort to come volunteer for you, be sure you have specific tasks for them to do, plenty of work in that task to do, and the tools they need to do it. Greet them when they arrive, act like you were expecting them, and show them to their already-set-up work station. If they are joining you out in the field, make sure you have them assigned to a specific task. If another staff member is heading up that task, be sure that person has a list of

> **Fun Fact**
> The nonprofit world celebrates National Volunteer Week in April each year. Check the Independent Sector website at independentsector.org for the dates for the next year.

the volunteers (this is where a specific volunteer coordinator comes in very handy) assigned to that station or task.

Volunteers typically don't expect to be coddled but they do appreciate that you remember they were coming to help and that you express that by having an assignment for them and what they need to complete that assignment.

Numbers

Once you have your lists organized, determine how many volunteers for each program you will need. To come up with a "job description" for each of those

You Don't Have to Start from Scratch

If your organization will utilize a lot of volunteers, you need volunteers with specific skills, or you need a few intensive volunteers, try reaching out to volunteer organizations such as AmeriCorps, United Way, or state organizations like VolunteerNH. These organizations provide a certain amount of screening. They may also widen your volunteer pool by allowing you to upload your specific project and its volunteer needs on a website that is viewed by potential volunteers who can apply directly to you.

AmeriCorps (and SeniorCorps and the Social Innovation Fund) are administered through the Corporation for National & Community Service (see their website at nationalservice.gov for complete information). CNCS's mission is to "improve lives, strengthen communities, and foster civic engagement through service and volunteering."

It's important to check out all of these potential volunteer-source sites—the nonprofit sector and volunteering has been around for a long time; there is no need to reinvent the wheel!

volunteer positions, think through the kinds of skill that the particular position will need. Is this a position that will put the volunteer in front of the public? Is it one that will require someone very detail oriented? Is this program going to require volunteers to staff booths at various events, which means at least a few volunteers are going to need to be able to do some moderately heavy lifting and toting of pop-up tents and bins of supplies?

Map out how many of each type of program you will do throughout a given period and begin recruiting the appropriate volunteers in both number and skill set.

Fun Fact

The American Red Cross mobilizes over a half million volunteers each year to help people around the world who are dealing with the aftermath of disasters. They have trained over 15 million volunteers who are ready for deployment in the event they are needed to assist in emergencies.

—"Roles of the Nonprofit and Philanthropic Community," *Independent Sector*

Youth versus Adult

Not all your volunteers need be adults. Youth love to volunteer, sometimes just because and sometimes because they can get school credit for their time. Check your state laws for minimum ages for volunteers in your state. Typically 12 years old is the cutoff, although some states may have a 14-year-old limit.

Your organization may want to impose its own age limit, depending on what type of work you do. Habitat for Humanity, for example, states that "for safety reasons, we are unable to accommodate youth under the age of 14" (habitatsa.org/volunteer/ageRegulations.aspx). All youth volunteers (under the age of 18) should be required to obtain parental/guardian signature on their application and should have adult supervision while volunteering.

Smart Tip

Don't forget that your board of directors is typically one of your key groups of volunteers! Be sure they track hours and get invitations to special volunteer appreciation events.

But just because a volunteer must be 14 years or older does not mean younger kids can't participate in your organization. This is where programming can step in. Perhaps there is a program you can create that helps younger students learn something about your organization and its mission while contributing to it—perhaps a craft project that teaches knitting to kids while they make baby caps as a project. Or they can create something for seniors to be delivered with their hot meals that might bring a smile to their faces around Halloween. Young kids can fully engage with your organization without technically clocking volunteer hours.

Programs

Since your volunteer corps can be a critical component in the ability of an organization to carry out its mission, which is often accomplished through programs, this is a good moment to discuss programming.

First and foremost, as you start up your organization, it is critical not to be overambitious in your plans for service or program delivery. Map out a plan for reaching the most ambitious goal that you aspire to; then work back and start at the other end to work your way up to your goal.

For example, if you are a statewide organization and want your services or programs available in every county in the state, start with one county, perhaps the county you know best. Set up your program in that one county, loking for ways to make these processes useable across all other counties as you expand. Think about it like you are setting up to franchise—only you will be franchising to yourself. But as you set up your programs and processes, keep things flexible enough to be able to adapt them for the differences you may find in other areas.

Starting small and working up will allow you to work out the kinks in the delivery of your programs and services while fixes are still at a manageable size.

Program Measurables

Once again, it is worth pointing out that while a nonprofit does not exist to make money, if it does not make money it will not exist. One way for a nonprofit to bring in income is from grants. Grant writers know that grant applications often ask about the measureable impact your nonprofit has on the community it serves. Set up systems right from the start that allow you to keep track of your program and service delivery so that you can extrapolate data that can express the impact your nonprofit has.

Perhaps you delivered a literacy program to pre-teen eighth graders at all the middle schools in one county; one measureable might be what percentage of those students went on to high school compared to the average for students graduating eighth grade and going on to high school in the rest of the state. Or maybe your measurable is even more directly related and shows that 100 percent of the students who went through your program tested at an eighth-grade reading level, while 75 percent of the students not in the program tested at a sixth-grade or below reading level. Those are strong numbers that clearly show the success of your program.

Be sure to build measurables into your program and service delivery so you can have a way to show the public and those handing out grant funding that your organization is having a positive impact and is a worthwhile investment. If you think about this after the fact, it is hard to re-create the information you might need.

Volunteer Heaven

Focus on volunteers as a key component to the health of your nonprofit. Choose carefully where you place volunteers—both where in your organization you utilize volunteers and which volunteers you put to what tasks. The more organized you are about your volunteer corps, the more likely you will have successful, productive volunteers who stay with your organization for a long time.

Equipping Your Nonprofit
Figuring Out What You Need to Run Your Shop and How to Get It

Certainly creativity is one of the most important pieces of "equipment" you'll need, but there are a number of more mundane machines that are essential to your operation. You don't need every single piece of equipment listed in this chapter to get started, but you should at least consider each one and decide how it works in relation to your own goals and growth strategy. (Refer to the equipment checklist on page 96 to help you get started.)

Equipment Choices

If you find a trip to the local office supply store fun and exciting, be careful not to get carried away when you're surrounded with an abundance of clever gadgets, all designed to make you think they will make your working life easier and more fun. Discipline yourself to get only what you need and really think through those "make your life easier" purchases that end up sitting in the back of the closet waiting for clean-out day. One thing nonprofits cannot afford to do is waste money.

On the other hand, do invest in equipment and supplies that make your organization professional and as high functioning as possible.

For example, although well-meaning people are apt to donate equipment to your cause rather than throw them away, are old computers with slow processors and out-of-date software really the best things to use to accomplish your goals? Donor databases take a lot of memory and require speed to work efficiently.

If you are of the size where printing out 300 letters for your membership renewal yourself is the better way to do a membership drive than to send it to a mail house, be sure to invest in a printer that has a high page-per-minute rate or a photocopier that efficiently uses toner, one of the most expensive parts of photocopying.

Basic Office Equipment

Here are some basic equipment purchases you should consider adding to your startup budget:

- *Computers.* A computer can help you manage complex bookkeeping tasks, maintain your donor database, and produce marketing materials. For well under $1,000 you can buy a desktop setup with 8GB

Smart Tip *Tip...*

When you acquire your donor database, consider doing it with a cloud-based software. This means you have access to your database anywhere you have internet service and the system is automatically updated by the software owner.

of memory and the most current processor available to the general consumer. Get a wireless system so everyone in the office can connect to the server and internet without cords. It is worth the cost to equip everyone on your staff with an up-to-date computer.

If you are an "Apple person" or envision doing a lot of graphic design for your nonprofit, you might decide to use an Apple system. This will be more costly, but the right tool for the job is less costly in the long run.

Beware!
Though integrated, multifunction devices—such as a copier/printer/fax machine or a fax/telephone/answering machine—may cost less to acquire and take up less space in your office, you risk losing all these functions simultaneously if the equipment fails. Also, consider your anticipated volume of use with the machine's efficiency rating and cost to operate and compare that with stand-alone machines before making a final decision.

- *Printers.* You could get one super-duper printer or have a more modest one with each computer. Everyone having their own printer at their desk can save a lot of jumping up and down time. A lot depends on the number of staff and the setup of the office. Perhaps having one more powerful printer attached to the administrative desk computer and simpler printers at each desk is a good solution. Small printers that do quite a lot are available for not much more than $100.

- *Software.* Be sure to get the latest version of Microsoft Office. The full suite includes Word, Excel, Access, Publisher, and PowerPoint. If you are starting very small, you could use Access or even Excel as your database until you get to a certain number of records, when you will want to transfer your data to a donor database.

  Software can be a significant investment, so do a careful analysis of your own needs, then study the market and examine a variety of products before making a final decision.

- *Photocopier.* A photocopier is a must. You can get a basic, low-end, no-frills personal copier for less than $400 in just about any office supply store. More elaborate models increase proportionately in price. If you anticipate a heavy volume, consider leasing. This is also a common area where someone might be willing to donate a lease of a photocopier to your organization; you just pay for the toner and monthly service. Most computer printers these days will also do photocopying, but use this feature sparingly since printer ink cartridges are even more costly than photocopier toner.

- *Fax machine.* Despite the widespread use of email, fax machines are still used by many. Depending on your organization's needs, a stand-alone machine on a dedicated telephone line can be a wise investment. Expect to pay $100 to $250 for a fax machine. If you are only receiving a fax or two a week maximum and are located near an office store that provides the service of receiving and sending faxes, it may not be worth purchasing a machine. Or perhaps you can get a local business to offer you free fax service for the small amount of faxing you may need.

- *Postage scale.* Unless all of your mail is identical, a postage scale is a valuable investment. An accurate scale takes the guesswork out of postage and will quickly pay for itself. It's a good idea to weigh every piece of mail to eliminate the risk of items being returned for insufficient postage or overpaying when you are unsure of the weight. This can save a lot of standing in line at busy post offices. Also, check www.USPS.com for doing online postage purchasing if you do any significant amount of mailing—and when all those donation checks start coming in, you will be sending regular thank-you letters!

- *Paper shredder.* A response to both a growing concern for privacy and the need to recycle and conserve space in landfills, shredders are becoming increasingly common in both homes and offices. They allow you to efficiently destroy incoming unsolicited direct mail, as well as sensitive internal documents before they are discarded. Shredded paper can be compacted much tighter than paper tossed in a wastebasket, and it can also be used as packing material. Light-duty shredders start at about $25, and heavy-capacity shredders run from $150 to $500.

Bright Idea

Rather than purchasing mail-processing equipment and doing the work in-house, consider outsourcing all or part of the labor involved in preparing large mailings. Check under "mailing services" in the Yellow Pages.

Bright Idea

Postage stamps come in a wide array of sizes, designs, and themes and can add an element of color, whimsy, and even thoughtfulness to your mail. Check with the USPS for the latest on having a special bulk mail stamp put on your large mailings.

Telecommunications

If you have a physical office with more than one person on staff, you will need a phone system. If not, you can get away with a cell phone just for yourself. Telecommunications technology seems to advance on a weekly basis. As you investigate the options in your areas, here are some specific elements to keep in mind:

- *Telephone.* A single voice telephone line should be adequate during the startup period. As you grow, you'll add more lines. Keep this in mind as you choose a package that allows for growth without having to start over in purchasing equipment.

  Your actual telephone itself can be a tremendous productivity tool, and most of the models on the market today are rich in features you will find useful. Such features include automatic redial, which redials the last number called at regular intervals until the call is completed; programmable memory for storing frequently called numbers; and a speakerphone for hands-free use. You may also want call forwarding, which allows you to forward calls to another number when you're not at your desk, and call waiting, which signals you that another call is coming in while you are on the phone. These services are typically available through your telephone company for a monthly fee.

  If you or your staff will be spending a great deal of time on the phone, consider a headset for comfort and efficiency. A cordless phone lets you move around freely while talking, but these units vary widely in price and quality, so research them thoroughly before making a purchase.

- *Voice mail.* Because your phone should never go unanswered, you need some sort of reliable answering device to take calls when you can't do it yourself. Whether you buy an answering machine (expect to pay $40 to $150 for one that is suitable to a business) or use a voicemail service provided through your telephone company (anywhere from $6 to $20 per month) is a choice you

---

Dollar Stretcher

Just about any type of secondhand business equipment can be purchased for a fraction of its original retail cost. Check the classified section of your local newspaper and ask new equipment dealers if they have trade-ins or repossessions for sale. Careful shopping for used items can save hundreds of dollars.

▲

must make depending on your personal preferences, work style, and budget needs.

- *Cellular phone*. Once considered a luxury, cellular phones have become standard equipment for personal and business purposes. Will you or anyone on your staff travel frequently and have a need for being in touch on the road? Consider getting key personnel a cell phone—multiple phone packages might be a cost-effective way to do this.

- *Toll-free number*. If you are targeting a customer base outside your local calling area, you may want to provide them with a toll-free number so they can reach you without having to make a long-distance call. Most long-distance service providers offer toll-free numbers and have a wide range of service and price packages. Shop around to find the best deal for you. These days, you may be able to rely on people having unlimited calling cell phone plans. Think through your incoming calling before deciding.

- *Email*. Email is a standard element in a company's communications package. It allows for fast, efficient, 24-hour communication. If you have email, check your messages regularly and reply to them promptly. Use tools such as Microsoft Outlook to organize your emails—you can quickly become overwhelmed!

Other Equipment

In addition to these basics, there are other items you may need, depending on your particular operation. They include:

- *Cash register*. For a retail operation, you need a way to track sales, collect money, and make change. You can do this with something as simple as a divided cash drawer and a printing calculator, or you can purchase a sophisticated, state-of-the-art point-of-sale system that is networked with your computer. Of course, the latter will cost somewhere between $1,200 and $5,000 per terminal and may not be a practical investment for a small startup nonprofit. A preferable option is an electronic cash register (ECR), which can range from $600 to $3,000, and can be purchased outright, leased, or acquired under a lease-purchase agreement. The newer ECRs offer such options as payment records to designate whether a customer paid by cash, check, or charge; department price groupings (appropriate for stores with multiple departments so you can separate the prices for items in each department); sign-in keys to help you monitor cashiers and clerks; and product price groups (which let you organize products as they are rung up) for tracking inventory more effectively.

Smart Tip

If your retail space and operation is of any size, consider hiring a retail manager who has retail experience. Even more creative, consider leasing out the retail operation to someone who would like to run it as a separate business. Be sure to check all tax laws and local laws first.

- *Credit and debit card processing equipment.* Simple imprint machines that you slide across the top of a credit card with embossed numbers are quickly becoming relics of the past—cards are increasingly being issued without embossed numbers—so don't think that you are getting a useful item if someone is giving these away or selling them cheap. If you are doing transactions on the road, at events off-site, consider using a swipe mechanism like Square Card (squareup.com) that plugs into your cell phone and uses your cell line to transmit the transaction.

Credit and debit card service providers are widely available, so shop around to understand the service options, fees, and equipment costs. Expect to pay about $500 for a "swipe" machine that reads the magnetic strip on cards. You'll also pay a transaction charge, which might be a flat rate (perhaps 20 to 30 cents) per transaction or a percentage (typically 1.6 to 3.5 percent or in excess of 4 percent for higher-end cards like American Express) of the sale.

Inventory

If you have a retail operation, you will need to deal with inventory. This can be the most fun part of having retail as part of your nonprofit, and it can be a huge headache.

Inventory Stocking

Go slow with ordering inventory. Excess inventory creates extra overhead, and that costs you money. Inventory that sits in your storeroom does not generate sales or profits—it shrinks your bottom line. Losses caused by excess inventory come in the form of:

- Debt service on loans to purchase the excess inventory
- Additional personal property tax on unsold inventory

▲

Equipment Checklist

Use the following checklist as a shopping guide to get your work space and store (if you have a retail operation) set up. Each item listed is not necessarily required before you start, but if you don't buy them now, you'll want to have them eventually. Much of this is available used; look for stores going out of business that are selling their fixtures as a great way to pick up some bargains for retail-specific display units.

Store Equipment/Fixtures (for retail operations)

❑ Special displays and related hardware   _____

❑ Display shelving   _____

❑ Cash register   _____

❑ Counter   _____

❑ Marking guns   _____

❑ Floor gondolas   _____

❑ Pegboard (5 to 10 panels)   _____

❑ Hooks   _____

❑ Showcases (1 or 2)   _____

❑ Wall gondolas (5 to 10)   _____

Packaging/Shipping Equipment

❑ Hand truck   _____

❑ High-speed tape dispenser   _____

❑ Carton stapler   _____

❑ Electronic scale   _____

❑ Paper shredder   _____

Office Furniture, Equipment, and Supplies

❑ Computer system (including printer)   _____

Equipment Checklist, continued

❑ Typewriter   _____

❑ Fax machine   _____

❑ Software   _____

❑ Phone system   _____

❑ Answering machine or voice mail   _____

❑ Uninterruptible power supply   _____

❑ Surge protector   _____

❑ Calculator/adding machine   _____

❑ Copier   _____

❑ Desk   _____

❑ Desk chair   _____

❑ Printer stand   _____

❑ File cabinet(s)   _____

❑ Bookcase   _____

❑ Computer/copier paper   _____

❑ Business cards   _____

❑ Letterhead-quality paper   _____

❑ Matching envelopes   _____

❑ Address stamp or stickers   _____

❑ Extra printer cartridge   _____

❑ Extra fax cartridge   _____

❑ Mouse pad   _____

❑ Miscellaneous office supplies   _____

Total Office Equipment and Furniture Expenditures   _____

- Increased insurance costs on the greater value of the inventory in stock

A common and natural reaction to excess inventory is to reduce the price and sell it quickly. While this may solve your overstocking problem, it also reduces your return on investment. All your financial projections assume that you will receive the full retail price for your goods. If you overstock and reduce your prices by 15 percent to 25 percent to jettison the excess inventory, you'll lose money you had counted on in budgeting.

You may be tempted to respond to the excess inventory issue with overly cautious reordering. But doing this risks creating a shortage in stock, and the result could be a drop in sales. The solution is to plan well to avoid accumulating excess inventory, establish a realistic safety margin, and order only what you're sure you can sell.

With nonprofits, one key parameter to use for ordering inventory may be how well it relates to your mission. If you are a museum, there are lots of related products—art, educational toys, and always books—that you can sell that make your retail store an extension of your museum.

Tracking Inventory

A critical part of managing inventory is tracking it—that means knowing what you have on hand, what's on order and when it will arrive, and what you've already sold. This information allows you to plan your purchases intelligently, quickly recognize fast-moving items that need to be reordered, and identify slow-moving merchandise that should be marked down and moved out.

There are a variety of inventory-tracking methods you can use, from basic handwritten records to computerized bar code systems. Your accountant can help you develop a system that will work for your particular situation.

Vehicles

Does your organization have the need for a vehicle? If you transport things on a regular basis or do events where you need to carry lots of equipment and supplies— like pop-up tents or tubs full of literature—you should consider whether having an organization-owned vehicle is logical. Employees using their own vehicles once in a while is fine, but if this is a regular thing—once or twice a week—a company vehicle may be important.

Begin to develop relationships with local car dealers and see if anyone is interested enough in your mission to help you with a great deal on a purchase, or even a donation. This is great publicity for a car dealer. However, cars do not bring in a lot of profit, so keep in mind this will likely be a dealer who is very committed to your organization.

Another option is to rent a vehicle from one of the major rental companies like Ryder or U-Haul or Enterprise, if this need is no more than once or twice a month.

Beware!

If you decide retail sales offer a great opportunity for your organization to make some operating funds, check carefully into IRS tax law regarding nonprofits selling retail. You may decide to have that portion of your operation pay sales/business taxes in order to be able to be as large as you want. But then be careful of local laws if your retail space is not on the property tax rolls.

Security

If you have set up shop within an existing operation, you may already be covered with a security system. However, if you are a stand-alone operation, you will need to consider what level of security you need to employ.

Do you have cash and donations sitting in your office most of the time? (That is a nice problem to have, but one you need to consider!) If large amounts of money are coming in daily, you need to have a plan for getting deposits in to the bank often. Consider having a locking safe for those times when it just adds up.

A security alarm tied into the local police dispatch is another key thing to have. Don't let people be lax about setting the alarm. Pick a system that isn't so complicated people hate to use it. Be meticulous about handing out security codes and keys and other security-related information. Keep records of who uses what code.

Keeping your establishment as secure as possible is a serious responsibility. The costs are not that high and well worth the peace of mind.

Talk with local police to help you determine what level of security you might need. Most will gladly provide free information on safeguarding your operation and will likely even personally visit your site to discuss specific crime-prevention strategies. If you have a retail operation where shoplifting may be a concern, check your local law enforcement department to see if it offers retailers and their employees training seminars in workplace safety and crime prevention.

▲

Common techniques merchants use to enhance security and reduce shoplifting include mirrors, alarms, and video monitors. Technology is bringing the cost of these items down rapidly, and installing them may also earn you discounts on your insurance. You can also increase the effectiveness of your security system by prominently posting signs in your windows and around the store announcing the presence of the equipment.

Beyond the Minimum

When setting up your nonprofit business, there is a balance to be sought to get the tools you need upfront while at the same time holding off on some things that you know you will need but will know better about the features you will want once you are up and running. The other balance is doing the research and purchasing while you are still in the planning stages. Once your nonprofit, whatever it is, is open for business, you will find it hard to find the time to do this kind of behind-the-scenes work!

9

Development
Raising the Funds
You Need

The term "development" in the nonprofit world, sometimes called "advancement" in the university setting, is the term used for the area of the organization that focuses on raising funds. The people of the United States are a philanthropic bunch; enough so that the IRS set up the 501(c)(3) designation and has a distinct interpretation of charitable giving (found on the website irs.gov/charities/index.html):

> The exempt purposes set forth in section 501(c)(3) are charitable, religious, educational, scientific, literary, testing for public safety, fostering national or international amateur sports competition, and preventing the cruelty of children or animals. The term *charitable* is used in its generally accepted legal sense and includes relief of the poor, the distressed, or the underprivileged; advancement of religion; advancement of education or science; erecting or maintaining public buildings, monuments, or works; lessening the burdens of government; lessening neighborhood tensions; eliminating prejudice and discrimination; defending human and civil rights secured by law; and combating community deterioration and juvenile delinquency.

That covers a lot of ground! But the point is that the IRS has recognized that people in this country want to help their fellow citizens and their communities through volunteering and charitable giving. Nonprofit leaders need to recognize that, too.

As you embark on starting up your nonprofit, if you—and your board and staff—get nothing else out of this book, get this: Do not go about fundraising with the attitude that you are begging people to donate. Realize that statistics show that people *want* to donate—and you are giving them a chance to understand your organization and decide whether it is a cause they are interested in supporting. People with means to donate money or time to volunteer want to do so with organizations that hold meaning to them. But they won't be able to pick your organization to add to their list of charitable giving if they don't know about you and your mission.

Staff

It is unlikely you will open your doors with a fully staffed development department. In fact, it is more likely that you as the founder and/or ED or chair of the board will be the fundraiser in chief. Whatever your title, the executive director, the board chair, and the board members will also need to be key fundraisers for the success of the organization. However, it is worth spending time on a plan for your development efforts and how to staff this important function.

A startup nonprofit with an involved founder and a high-functioning board doesn't need a high-level development staff member right off the bat. Unless you are launching your startup with a massive capital campaign—which isn't recommended, or, if you do, can be accomplished with a consultant/contractor whose role is not to be a permanent member of the staff but to conduct the campaign for you—your first key development hire likely should be for an administrative role.

An administrative assistant or development assistant/associate is critical for timely mail processing, updating the donor database, and generating acknowledgment letters. These three functions alone can easily be a thirty-hour/week job for even small nonprofit organizations.

Adding development staff should be a slow process. There are ways to get development-related work done on a consultant or even volunteer basis. You can hire a grant writer on an hourly, by-project basis. As mentioned above, for something with a beginning and end point like a capital campaign to build or renovate a building or launch a large new initiative, you can hire a consultant with a set contract for that project. But if your organization is going to grow even slowly, you will want to hire development staff to focus on your specific needs. Here are a few of the development tasks that are often separate jobs in bigger organizations.

Development Assistant

If you, as founder, or your executive director or your board president (and especially all three!) are fundraising savvy, a development assistant is a great first hire for the start of a development department in a small startup organization. The salary level is not high, you don't need someone with development-specific skills, and this person will be invaluable for keeping administrative tasks flowing and helping support the fundraising efforts of your key personnel.

The development assistant can be a move-up position, which is often a great way to retain someone and not have to retrain people to your organization regularly. As he or she gains specific knowledge of your organization, your donors, your prospects, and your database, your development assistant will be a great candidate to move up through the ranks to development coordinator to development associate to development manager and eventually to development director.

Membership Coordinator

This person would organize your membership efforts, if you are a membership-based organization. Membership coordinating involves soliciting members with mailings, keeping track of membership in the database, sending renewal notices, coming up with tantalizing benefits (besides supporting your good work), and making sure members receive the benefits and premiums you offer. Also, members should be communicated with regularly—even if that is done by a communications director, the membership coordinator should provide copy for the member newsletter and produce or remind someone to produce eblasts, etc.

Special Events Manager

If special events are a huge part of your fundraising efforts, keep in mind that they are also a huge amount of work. If you plan to do several events a year, you will want to look toward having someone on staff who is dedicated to events. Large events can raise a lot of money, so this position can ultimately pay for itself. You will likely start with volunteer committees with a key staff person being the lead for each event, but as your organization grows and your events grow or you do more events, don't burn out your staff, but bring on either a special events contractor to run the event or hire someone in development who focuses on events.

Other Personnel

There are loads of other potential development hires if your organization gets large enough that these elements of your fundraising efforts represent a full-time (or significant part-time) workload.

Direct Mail Coordinator

Your "annual appeal," membership solicitation, newsletter, and other appeals that go through the mail or through email are part of your direct-mail effort. Depending on the size and/or number of mailings you do, coordinating your direct mail can be a standalone job. You can hire an outside direct mail firm to coordinate this or you can have a dedicated staff person working on developing creative mailings and pulling together lists of prospects.

Grant Writer

Typically people within the organization work on grant proposal writing as they have time, but if grants are a key piece of your fundraising efforts or if you depend on large government grants that can be very complicated to pull together, you may want to hire an on-staff grant writer. Grant writing requires more than just good writing—however, most good grant writers are good writers, so you could add some general writing tasks to this position to get the most out of this staff member in downtimes between grant proposal deadlines.

Volunteer Coordinator

This is discussed in more detail in Chapters 6 and 7 on staff and volunteers, but if your organization depends heavily on volunteers, it may pay to have a volunteer coordinator. This not only ensures that volunteers are where they are needed, but it also ensures that your volunteers are getting the most out of their volunteer effort, a key ingredient to heavily utilizing volunteers in any organization.

Donor Databases

A database is simply a collection of information stored electronically, which can be manipulated or retrieved using a computer program. There are a few key things to keep in mind about the database kept by your organization:

1. *Garbage in, garbage out.* This is the simple saying that states that if the information entered into the database is inaccurate, the reports and lists that you ask the database to produce will also be inaccurate and not as useful as they could be.

2. *Databases used by nonprofit development departments are known as "donor databases."* Unlike bookkeeping software/databases, they do not revolve around money; they revolve around people—people's names, donations, and relationships to other people.

3. *Be sparing in the number of people you allow to enter information into the database.* Database software typically appoints an "administrator" who can change anything about the database that is allowed to be changed by the user (as opposed to the software developer)—add/delete/alter fields or add users and decide what level of use those users will have. Development personnel should have full access once trained. Other personnel should have access as needed—for example, the ED should probably have full

Smart Tip

Don't rely only on on-the-job training to move your development assistant up the ladder. Budget a small professional development fund to get this person outside training that will help them understand the whole development picture.

▲

access (although watch out for those EDs who don't fully understand the donor database!), while receptionists should have access to the database to view records (for phone numbers, addresses, etc.) but not to change unless you want to set them up to change contact information if they receive new information from a caller.

Most of the major donor databases link up with QuickBooks bookkeeping software to help coordinate the donation processing with the finances of your organization.

Which to Buy?

There are dozens of companies that make donor databases. This is a key purchase for your organization (and, depending on what you choose, will exceed $10,000 in cost), so before purchasing the database for your organization, you should fully assess how you plan to use it and how big and how fast you expect your organization to grow. A startup is unlikely to have the budget to buy the top-of-the-line donor database; but if you plan to grow exponentially within, say, five years, it might be best to just go with the most robust database out there since switching in five years is an expensive proposition, not only in purchase price but in personnel training and learning curve time.

Here are a couple of the donor databases out there at the moment:

- *The Raiser's Edge.* Owned by Blackbaud, The Raiser's Edge is considered among the cream of the crop of donor databases. It has the capability of managing large amounts of data, thousands of records, and providing detailed reports. If your organization is in one of the large categories like medical, research, or education, or if you expect your organization to start pretty small but grow pretty big pretty fast, you should seriously consider this development software.

- *DonorPerfect.* From SofterWare, this is another robust program that can manage tens of thousands of records and help not only keep track of your incoming donations, members, and other donation and donor tracking, but provide reports and lists, generate acknowledgments, and track contact with donors.

DonorPro (from TowerCare.com), GiftWorks (GiftWorksConnect.com), eTapestry (also from Blackbaud at www.blackbaud.com/etapestry) and dozens of others are all possibilities. Check out rlweiner.com for a long list by consultant Robert L. Weiner of donor databases. This is just a list, so you will need to do your own research—and remember, companies are being bought and sold all the time, so make sure the research you find is up to date.

Types of Donors

As your organization develops, you will find that you don't have just one type of donor. Each type will come with different ways that they want to be engaged and have differing ways that you will want to steward them to keep them contributing to your organization. And even these key donor types break down into further categories of donors.

Prospects

Prospects are people who you enter into your donor database who have not yet donated but are prime candidates for supporting your organization in some way, large or small. They are people that you want to make sure receive your mailings, from your quarterly newsletter to your annual appeal. Some day when the right pieces come together—extra money in their pocket or a personal connection to your mission—prospects have a high likelihood of sending you a donation.

Individual Donors

Individual donors come to donate to your organization for myriad reasons. Perhaps they came to an open house or other event you held, were impressed with the event and your organization, and donated beyond just the admission fee. They may have become a member or donated to a specific cause being showcased by the event.

Perhaps your individual donor responded to a direct-mail piece that was sent to ten thousand households. Your appeal spoke to an interest of theirs, they were impressed with your statistics, or they remembered a friend of theirs saying that they were a member of your organization and really appreciated what you do and the person donated a small amount for that reason alone.

Basically, "individual donors" will collectively be the lifeblood of your donor base. No one individual donation brought in this way is going to make or break your organization, but together they form a large percentage of your annual operating income.

These donors will likely donate, perhaps in just small amounts, again and again. They will respond to your membership appeal, they will come to other events, and they will donate to a special appeal for something specific.

These small, regular donors are also often the ones you will be surprised to find left your organization a substantial sum in their will.

Major Donors

Major donors rarely happen overnight. They might take years of cultivation, but once they decide to give, they give in large sums. Some may have the capacity to give a large sum annually, some may give only strategically when you are doing a special campaign.

Cultivation and, once they have given, stewardship is important to the major donor. They don't want to be "sold to" but they also want to be kept apprised of what your organization is doing—i.e., how you are using their donation.

One of the best ways to steward major donors is to assign each one to the most suitable board member. It is likely many of the major donors came through board member connections to begin with. Help your board members learn how to best steward donors if they don't already know. A plan should be in place for each major donor to receive a certain amount of correspondence each year—not asking for a donation but simply updating them on key initiatives or the overall status of the organization.

When the time comes to ask for a key donation, the board member should plan to bring along the executive director or development director for a face-to-face meeting.

Corporate Donors

Corporate donors require a completely different approach than individual and major donors. Although they certainly do exist, few corporations give large donations simply to be philanthropic. They expect certain marketing opportunities from their donation—a press release announcing a significant gift, a check presentation photo sent to the papers, naming of a key area in the building to which they are giving, publicity for sponsorship donations before, during, and after an event.

Corporations should be key donors and donor prospects in any organization's development plan. The board should be enlisted to help identify corporations for whom your mission would appeal. Corporations don't just donate for their own/

owner's sake; also help them understand that your organization's mission is near and dear to the hearts of their employees.

You will want to figure out the fiscal year for the corporations you plan to approach as much as possible. As you try to gather this information, you might consider creating a corporate mailing piece that can be sent a couple of times a year to a certain number of corporations. Once you start to collect specifics about their fiscal year, you can group those twice–a-year mailings by the most logical mailing period for a company's fiscal year.

And remember, corporations will be doing budgeting for the new fiscal year several months before the current year ends.

Foundations

Private foundations are pots of money set aside by a person, family, or other entity for donation purposes. They typically fall under tax-free IRS laws which, for the tax-free status, require them to give away a certain amount of money—typically a percentage of the income or the principal of the fund itself, depending on how it is set up—each year. In order to do that, they often target types of charities they are interested in and open a grant proposal round once or twice a year during which organizations can appeal to them for funding.

Foundations often prefer to fund programs that actually result in accomplishing the mission of the organization. Few foundations offer funding to capital campaigns, and fewer tend to offer funding of general operating funds for the day-to-day business of the organization. Most require a post-grant report to give them the measurables that show how their funding helped you to accomplish your mission.

There are many ways of finding out who offers grant funding in your category of charity. Do a basic search under "grants for" whatever your category is and you will come up with some places to start.

Grant Writing

Writing grant proposals is an important element of any development plan. However,

Smart Tip

Tip...

In-kind donations should receive letters acknowledging their gifts but the letter should not include a value; that is determined by the owner unless the donation is specific, like a gift card. But be sure to estimate in-kind donation values and enter them in your database to account for them in your annual income tallies.

do not overestimate the percentage of your funding that will come from grants. GivingUSA reported that in 2011, just 14 percent of nonprofit funding came from grants while 73 percent came from individual giving. That is a key ratio to keep in mind when thinking about how big a role grant proposal writing should play in the development plan of any nonprofit organization.

Some nonprofit categories have more potential grant funding than others. Health and human service nonprofits likely have a higher percentage of government grants available to them. In individual sectors, there are particular grant funding opportunities, but the grant amounts may make it impossible for the grant writing of the proposals to take up too much of limited staff time. This can be an area where a freelance grant writer could take up the slack. Plan to pay an hourly fee, however; it is considered unethical for a grant writer to take a percentage of the grant amount.

Events

Fundraising through events is extremely common in the nonprofit world. Open a weekly newspaper and you will find any number of local events being put on by nonprofits. Events are great. They engage your constituents and allow people to become involved with supporting your organization at almost any level.

The kinds of events most often put on by nonprofits include:

- Runs and walks where participants pay a certain set amount to enter but also are encouraged to obtain other donations from friends, family, and colleagues. Many online nonprofit fundraising programs—such as Razoo and FirstGiving—also have the ability for people to set up their own fundraising pages on behalf of your organization.

- Dinners that might include a speaker, live and silent auctions, and other clever ways to earn money from the event beyond the price paid to have dinner

- Online auctions—again, several online donation programs also have the ability to conduct auctions for your organization; they often have

Smart Tip

Use a capacity screening tool such as Wealth Engine or Prospect Builder to analyze the giving capacity of potential donors. These tools help you understand ahead of the "ask" how much the donor is likely to be comfortable giving, what might be a stretch, and what would be too big of an ask.

great tips on how to obtain auction items and the best items to obtain.

- Holiday-themed events such as haunted houses, Santa events, New Year's galas, fall festivals, Valentine's Day chocolate-related activities, and many other possibilities

- Casino trips, bus tours, etc., are all great fun, can be great publicity, and many can be great fundraisers. But you need to weigh the pros and cons of how much the event can make compared to how much staff time and other expenses cost, as well as how much time is being taken away from other types of fundraising.And at what point are you doing more event planning than serving your mission?

Earned Income

Earned income refers to fees charged for services you offer or revenue from goods your organization sells. If your nonprofit is the type that has a physical space, then having some amount of retail is probably a good idea. Patrons of museums want and expect at least a small museum store where they can purchase souvenirs of their visit, postcards of their favorite piece of art in your museum, or simply high-quality and unusual gift items.

Be careful of earned income and keep track of the percentage of your organization's income that is through goods and services; there are lots of variables, but the IRS has very specific rules on how much of a nonprofit's income can be earned before you no longer are operating like a charitable organization.

Stat Fact
Only 4 percent of all nonprofit organizations spend in excess of $10 million, but these organizations represent 85 percent of all nonprofit spending.
—*The Nonprofit Almanac 2012*

And people should know that this is not a charitable donation to your organization that they can write off on their taxes; it is a purchase like any other.

Annual Appeal

A nonprofit's annual fund is that into which "unrestricted" donations go, i.e., given without any restrictions as to what the donations are used for but instead go into the organization's general pot of money called "operating funds." This is considered the best kind of donation a nonprofit can get—the kind of donation that allows the leaders of the nonprofit to decide where the best place is to use the donation given what the organization most needs at that moment in time.

The annual fund is raised through a direct appeal out to the widest possible audience—from known regular donors to occasional donors to haven't-yet-donated prospects. This appeal usually goes out in direct-mail format in the late fall, hitting people in their mailboxes at the holidays when they are feeling the most generous and are looking ahead to the end of the calendar year and the benefit of a tax deduction.

Appeal Letter

The annual appeal will have several components. The letter is the key piece around which the appeal is built. Don't be afraid of your letter being a few paragraphs long. While the general thinking is that people do not read these days, in fact statistics show that these letters are read. And, speaking of statistics, Mark Pittman in his blog on FundraisingCoach.com reminds writers of appeal letters to keep statistics out of their letters. Potential donors want anecdotes about the good work your organization does; they do not know what to do with statistical information, which is often a rather random set of impersonal numbers that are meaningful only to those involved in the industry in which your organization sits. Tell stories, show pictures, talk about what your organization did over the past year, and what it plans to do in the upcoming year.

Be careful of creating too slick of a mailing piece that gives the impression that you are spending donors' money on creating mailing pieces soliciting donations. You want to look professional and create a design that is in keeping with the type of organization you are in—a mailing piece from a private school is going to want to look quite a bit different from a mailing piece from an animal shelter, for example. However, that doesn't mean the animal shelter mailing piece shouldn't look professional or that the private academy's piece shouldn't look personal!

Remittance Envelope

The standard way to provide a convenient means for returning their donation is to provide a self-addressed remittance envelope—a "remit" envelope. This is the little envelope with the large flap that has on the inside printed check boxes with standard donation amounts and lines for credit card information. They make it out, put their

Stat Fact

The Charitable Remainder Trust planned giving tool was made possible through the Tax Reform Act of 1969. It allows an investment to be transferred to a trust on behalf of a charity but from which the donor can receive income while still alive or for a set period of time.

—CharitableRemainderTrust.com
FAQ page

check in, seal it, stamp it, and send it. These tend to be more expensive than standard No. 9 return envelopes, but they can be worth it.

Buckslip

If you do not provide a remit envelope but use a simple self-addressed envelope, you will need to provide a separate slip to be included with the donation that will have the same information on it as would be on the remit envelope flap. The donor would write a check or write their credit card info on that buckslip, put it in the No. 9 return envelope, seal, stamp, and send.

You can also distinguish your appeal by adding a photo and "sell line" to the outside of the mailing envelope to encourage people to open the envelope to see what you have to say, rather than just throw it away without reading it.

Membership

If your organization is such that membership makes sense, by all means, offer membership. This is yet another type of funding appeal and can bring in much-needed funds either throughout the year or at a time frame during the year when you are not doing another appeal.

Membership Timing

Rolling membership refers to when the membership renewal is one year from the date of joining. This means that membership income is coming in at almost every month of the year. It also means that someone has to be sending out renewal notices all year long. This sounds ominous, but even the simplest database can help keep track of this.

Memberships that are renewed on a one-time-of-the-year basis get an appeal-type mailing. The advantage to this is that you can time your membership appeal to bring in donations at a time of the year other than your annual appeal, helping your cash flow. A key disadvantage is that it is easy to forget about membership at other times of the year, resulting in often not capturing members who have let their membership lapse for a couple of months. And you may be losing new members who find out about you and your membership opportunity in April, but your membership renewal is once a year in September. They may not want to join in April for just a few months but decide to wait until September—but they aren't in your database and they forget and so they never join.

Only you can decide which approach is best for your organization; just weigh the pros and cons of each.

Planned Giving

Planned giving gets the classic brush-aside. No one wants to talk about planned giving—that means talking about death. And who wants to talk about that?

The best way to get over that is to stop approaching it as a talk about death. Approach planned giving as an opportunity for donors who care about your organization to have a lasting positive impact on your organization. Many nonprofits call their planned giving campaign a "Legacy Society." People are quite interested in leaving a legacy in an area they care about deeply.

If you can get a couple of people who have named your organization in their will to step forward and say so publicly, that is the best awareness campaign you can have. Often board members are willing to do that. Recognize legacy gifts that you are made aware of in some way—perhaps an annual lunch for Legacy Society members, a special pin, a beautifully framed picture of a special tract of land your organization protected, or a limited edition image of your museum. It should be something that is not expensive but is meaningful to the donor.

Bequests and planned gifts such as beneficiary to insurance policies, etc., can be turning point gifts for any organization. They can provide unrestricted funds at just the right moment, perhaps provide purchase funds for a piece of land for your future new facility or the seed money for an endowment that you can launch a capital campaign to contribute to.

Tip...

Smart Tip
You don't ask for the donation the first time you meet with the potential donor. The point at which you request support and the amount you put forward is known as *the ask*. There are key cultivation strategies leading up to the ask.

Whatever you do with planned giving, do not ignore the benefits of this type of gift to both you and the donor. Planned giving tools are not as complicated as people think. Consider hosting a workshop conducted by a lawyer who specializes in planned giving to help your constituents understand these tools: from wills, to charitable remainder trusts, to insurance policy named beneficiaries.

Capital Campaigns

A capital campaign refers to a campaign to generate donations for a specific initiative, such as a new building on campus, a new facility to replace your aging one, or a new large-scale program. The campaign is typically of a finite time period, designated by either when you collect the targeted sum or a specific time frame.

Capital campaigns for buildings can carry a certain amount of "naming rights." For a designated-sized donation, the donor will get some predetermined aspect of the new building named for them. An extremely large donation can get the entire building named—most higher education institutions or private schools have many buildings named after people who donated substantial sums. Programs get named as well. From there, you can bring it down to naming individual classrooms and benches in the courtyard. Donors often enjoy having their name physically attached to their passion and it gives them a specific sum to considering donating.

Silent Phase

The so-called "silent phase" of a capital campaign is critical. This is the phase when board members and the director and anyone else who has been a member of the steering committees cultivate individual and corporate donors to contribute to the campaign early in a substantial way. These donations set up the success of the "public phase" of the campaign.

Public Phase

This is the phase of a capital campaign where you go public with your plans and your monetary goal and announce the support you have already received in the silent phase. This is where it becomes clear how critical the silent phase is—this is the support that gives your general donor pool confidence that the campaign will succeed and is worthwhile.

Gift Pyramid

Before you begin your capital campaign, you should create a "gift pyramid." You can visually represent this as an actual pyramid or simply list the donation amounts and number of donors.

At the top of the gift pyramid are the largest donations, which will have the fewest number of donors. At the bottom of the pyramid are the largest number of donors and the smallest donations.

Say you want to raise $100,000. To get there, you think you have a pool of large donors that will likely result in two $25,000 donations. There's $50,000 of your $100,000.

Of this remaining $50,000, you think you could get two $10,000 donations. So there's

> **Smart Tip**
>
> If you are soliciting large donations for a building campaign, there can be obvious "naming opportunities" to attach to a gift size—*give $50,000 and get your name or your company's name posted next to our training room.*

$60,000. Perhaps you know a pool of donors from whom you feel you can secure four $5,000 donations. Now you are at $80,000. The next level is $1,000 donors and you are pretty certain there are ten of those in your pool of prospects. There's $90,000. The remaining $10,000 will likely be random smaller donations from $500 down to the person who wants to participate but can manage to donate only $25. There will be dozens of those—and that's OK; you definitely want to embrace them as much as any other donors.

The gift pyramid is not just a guess but is based on solid research done with donor capacity databases as well as the anecdotal knowledge of the teams of people you have put together to help with your campaign.

Acknowledgment

All donations should be acknowledged. You may want to set up a system whereby large donations are acknowledged immediately with a personal note and followed up by an official tax letter when the donation has made it through the bookkeeping system. Your general thank-you with a paragraph that says something like "The Appliance Museum is a 501(c)(3) corporation, EIN #00–0000000. No goods or services were received in exchange for this donation, which is tax deductible to the extent allowed by law."

> ## Beware!
>
> If you hire a seasoned development professional, let her or him use their experience! Founders often know a lot about their organization's mission, but development pros know a lot about how to get people on board with the mission in a meaningful way.

Letters

Even the most basic database should be able to generate your acknowledgment letters based on donation data input. Despite even the most systematic letter generation, you should always look through letters before they get mailed. Set up a system whereby letters can be personalized if someone sends a special note with their donation.

Email

Most donor databases offer a system for sending acknowledgments via email. Of course, the usefulness of this depends on how many emails are in your database. Many donors these days want to save paper and postage and are happy with email acknowledgments.

Memorial Donations

Many people donate in memory of a loved one or a friend they knew cared about your organization or your organization's mission. These days, many obituaries include "in lieu of flowers" suggestions that people who knew the deceased might wish to donate to a nonprofit of special interest to the person who has died or an organization somehow related to their death, like the American Heart Association for someone who died of a heart attack.

Memorial donations require not only a special letter specifying to whom their donation is in memory, but you also need to send a letter to the next of kin notifying them of the donations received in memory of their loved one. Most sophisticated donor databases allow you to track memorial donations and generate a report with a list of all donations in memory of a specific person, which can be inserted into a letter to next of kin.

Do not underestimate the importance of these letters, and be sure to set up a system and time frame to generate them in a timely fashion.

In-Kind Donations

In-kind donations—donations of goods and services, not cash—are donations that are tracked in your donor database. Be sure to set up a system for these donations to be

▲

tracked when they are given. Acknowledgment letters typically do not mention a value of in-kind donations but let the donor decide what the goods were worth. However, you will want to record in your database some "fair market value" of your in-kind donations for bookkeeping purposes. Estimate the value of products; keep a list for things that you receive as in-kind donations regularly.

Fundraising Is King

The development function in any nonprofit organization is clearly a critical one. While few nonprofits can afford to have a large development staff—and certainly not right out of the box—this is one area where adding staff can have significant payoffs. However, be sure that your nonprofit promotes the notion that **every** staff member is a fundraiser for the organization, whether they are directly soliciting donations or simply helping people feel good about your nonprofit and your mission.

10

Master of Your Domain
Website Essentials

Although Facebook and other social media platforms are offering new and creative ways to reach out to constituents, there is no substitute yet for the good "old-fashioned" website. A well-thought-out website with a design that reflects your organization's style is a must.

Here are some basic things to keep in mind about a website for your organization:

- Websites give you the ability to change content quickly and cheaply, making it easy to keep the information about your organization up to date. Printing a brochure does not afford you that ease of change—in order to keep costs down, brochures need to be printed in high numbers, meaning you may still have hundreds left when you want to change something on it. Be sure to make use of a website's flexibility by regularly making changes and updates.

- Current and potential donors, volunteers, and other constituents can readily get information, or more information, on your organization just by looking at your website.

- You can track the results of your marketing efforts more easily with website "hits," questions, and donations you get from your site.

- You are open 24/7/365.

Mobile Websites

Mobile device-friendly websites have been around for a while. With the use of smartphones for web searching continuing to increase, and the closer we get to the wrist-worn smartphone, the world is on the verge of a yet another paradigm shift in the way we use computers. Creating a website that is more easily viewed on these devices can be a smart move.

Many people still choose to download the entire website no matter what device they are using, so if you don't want to spend the money on having a separate site created, it's not the end of the world. However, the more easily used your website is, the more you will spread the word about your organization and perhaps the more donations you will get.

Stat Fact
Mashable reports that if someone posts about a charity on Facebook, 68 percent of their Facebook friends are likely to investigate that charity further, 39 percent would actually donate, and 38 percent would repost the donation request to their Facebook friends.

Setting Up a Website

If you are adept at using a computer and want to design your own website, that's great, especially if it's going to be an information-only site that won't need the complications of interactive features.

However, no matter who designs your website, you need to be sure it is professional looking. Just like when you are meeting a potential constituent in person, you need your website to express your organization's style and culture. Check out all the websites of different organizations in your same category and get a sense of how their site caters to their base. Your website needs to do the same.

If you don't feel like you can create the right website, consider hiring a professional web design company. The cost is not necessarily out of reach, but you want to be sure to hire a company with the ability to do what you want it to do. You will also incur monthly charges to have it "hosted"—someone with a large server who keeps everything coming and going. Hosting fees can range from as little as $30 a month to several hundred, depending on the complexity of your web business.

Usually included in the hosting fee is a certain amount of monthly changes. However, it is highly recommended that you learn to make changes within your organization, even if it requires sending a staff person to a class to learn HTML or whatever language your website operates with. Internet users today expect websites to be dynamic. If your hours change seasonally, if your organization provides information and you want to be able to upload new articles and papers, or if you are constantly running new events, keeping your website up to date with all this new information is critical.

Before you hire a designer, look at lots of other websites and give the designer ideas on what you like and don't like. Your designer will likely provide you with a few options that you can choose from, either in their entirety or plucking bits and pieces from each.

Find web designers by searching online or noticing who designed the sites you like. The designer doesn't have to be local to design your site—everything can be done, well, online!

You can also buy "template" web designs—you fill the details into a basic design. There are many template companies to choose from, such as weebly.com, web.com, wordpress.org, or baskweb.com, which includes a shopping cart system. You don't have to be a computer programming wiz as they are designed to be put together by

Tip...

Smart Tip

Using a template doesn't mean you need to or should create a cookie cutter website—creative and changing content will make your site stand on its own.

▲

anyone with basic computer skills. Some wireless networks offer the ability to create a website through them. GoDaddy and other domain hosting sites also have templates, although they may cost a modest fee to use.

But if your organization is a little complex and you want to attract sophisticated donors to a contemporary, user-friendly, useable website, pay the price for having one designed by a professional. There might even be grant money out there to help fund the project! (See more in Chapter 9 on fundraising.)

The design of your site should be simple yet comprehensive. By the time people have spent a few minutes on your website, they should have a pretty good sense of your organization—your mission, your history, who your board members are, your goals, and the services you provide.

As a nonprofit organization, your website absolutely must contain easy, accessible, visible ways for potential donors to donate right then and there. If you have compelling text and present a professional appearance, visitors will want to donate. You don't want them to go away wishing they could have contributed to your cause. Donation boxes and online donation services (more on those later) capture emails and/or addresses that allow you to get an impulse donation as well as add them to your donor database and keep them apprised of what their donation is supporting.

Website Must-Haves

As you create your website, these are "must-haves":

- Homepage
- "Contact Us" page
- "About Us" page
- Testimonials from donors. Use real names (only with permission), not initials after the quotes, if possible. Try to get a couple of people who have chosen to include your organization in their will or other legacy gifts, if possible—a great seed to plant for viewers who might never have thought of this.
- Photos (make sure you have permission from not only the people shown but from the photographer)
- Your organization's logo, and address if there is any reason people might want to come visit your location, should appear on all of the pages of your website—don't make people dig for the basic information they want/need or to figure out whose website they are on.

And while we will discuss this in more detail later in this chapter and it is mentioned in Chapter 9 on development/fundraising, it is important enough to mention here as well: You should have a separate tab or page to donate—call it "how you can help" or "ways to donate" or whatever—but be sure it is there and easily found.

Smart Tip

Tip...

There is no quicker way to undermine your credibility than to maintain a sloppy website. Be sure that words are not misspelled. Misspelled words reflect carelessness and a lack of professionalism. It's worth spending a few bucks to pay someone to proofread your site before going live.

The Homepage

Viewers will first come to your homepage, where you will introduce them to your organization and tempt them to spend some time on your site browsing other pages—and ultimately be enticed enough to donate, join, or leave their contact information so you can start to cultivate them as a potential member, donor, volunteer, or however you hope to further engage them with your organization.

Your introduction should include history about how your organization got started; if you have a compelling story to tell that is meaningful and poignant, by all means tell it. But if your story is relatively simple, keep this information simple as well. This is a chance for people to feel like they understand your organization, but don't go into such detail that you lose them right at the homepage!

Avoid being too clever. The web customer should open to your site and immediately know they got what they are looking for. Be sure your organization name and contact information is right there. And be sure pictures of the highest quality showcase what your organization is all about—the interior of your museum, children receiving medical care, pets being happily adopted by a new family, hikers in a forest protected from development forever by your land trust organization.

You don't need and don't want to show everything you do right at the start. The web page might take too long to download to the viewer's electronic device, which will frustrate them enough to move on to the next thing they are interested in before they ever get captivated by your organization. Keep the homepage simple but informative.

By all means, do some promoting on this page—something that clearly reminds the viewer that you are a nonprofit with a mission and that they can help with that mission. How often you change this page depends on what setup you have with your website provider. You do want to keep the details of the homepage fresh, but you want the basic look to remain the same—viewers should immediately know they came to your site and should recognize it when they arrive on your homepage again.

Include a menu of items along one edge of your homepage—top or either side—with headings that the viewer can click on to get to that section of your site. Think of it like the signs you see overhead in the grocery store or the pharmacy—direct people to the sections they are interested in. The person

who came to your site to see what your next event is may or may not be interested in your organization's current advocacy projects. Make it easy for the website visitor to find what is particularly relevant to them—these are the ways you can keep them interested in your organization.

Drilling Down

Each time the viewer clicks a button on your website they get further into your site. This can be accomplished in two ways—one is with a "pop-up window" where, when they click on a category, the new section pops up over the main page and when they are finished browsing and close it out, ending up at the page they started from. The other "drills" them further and further into your site. Drilling down like this is a common way that websites are set up but it can get frustrating if the user can't easily get back to a point where they saw something they wanted to

look at further. One way to help this is to always have a "home" link/button on every page—all they have to do is click "home" to get them back to the beginning and find their way forward again from there. It's like having Dorothy's ruby red slippers on your site at all times—unlike for poor Dorothy, make sure it's clear how easy it is to get home without having to deal with flying monkeys and sleep-inducing poppies before getting there.

The Rest of the Site

Your homepage is one of the most important parts of your website. If you don't capture your visitors at the homepage, they are unlikely to go any further than that. But if your homepage does what it needs to do, viewers landing there will be intrigued enough by your photos and your text to move to the other areas of your site.

You might include a button for each area of your organization or for each service you provide. The homepage for The Texas Land Conservancy, for example, has buttons running across the top of the page that take visitors to information about the background of the TLC, the work they do, the lands they've protected, how you can get involved, or how you can support the Texas Land Conservancy. Decide what is best for your organization and what you want to promote.

Most websites will have their category buttons running across the top since they will all appear when you open the site and won't run off the bottom of the page. If you only have a few categories, then that might not be an issue. Whatever you do, be sure to design for ease of use and not just for looks.

> **Smart Tip** *Tip...*
>
> Always include your business's name, address, and phone number on every page of your website. Once customers have drilled a few pages down into your site, they don't want to have to backtrack all the way to your homepage just to get your contact information.

Contacting You from a Website

There was a time when websites were mainly marketing and information pieces—people came to the site to view what you do and offer, then called to talk with you directly. For nonprofit organizations, that is still an important role for the website. However, with the ease of use of today's technology, keep in mind that people are often browsing websites at 11:00 at night—they can't call you and speak to you then! If they have an impulse to donate to your organization or contact you for any reason, it should be possible to do that directly from your website.

For simple contact, be sure to have an email button—a separate one for each key member of your staff would be best. If you decide to have only one direct email contact, be sure to have a mechanism in place to communicate to other staff members about emails directed toward their function within the organization.

Beware!

Few things will make a visitor click away from a website faster than finding outdated information. Keep anything that is time sensitive up to date and regularly change anything that makes your site appear dated, such as reference to an event long past.

The Donate Button

The key thing about the donate button is to have one. It should be highly visible on your home page, it should be on other pages, and your site should have a drop-down menu with buttons for each way an interested person can donate—through membership, to a capital campaign (which you should call "The Building Fund" or something more generally understood than the phrase "capital campaign"), for a specific program, or just a general donation.

You get a donate button via the service you choose to process electronic donations. Most everyone is familiar with PayPal, the transaction service bought by eBay in 2002. PayPal charges a fee per online transaction—and offers approximately half a percentage point lower to nonprofits than what they charge for-profit businesses. Anyone with an email account can pay via PayPal; no PayPal account is needed. Payment is attached to a credit card.

Another online donation platform is Razoo. Razoo has a flat fee for processing your online contributions. Razoo is a platform especially helpful in setting up donor pages, where constituents encourage others to donate to their donor page on the behalf of your organization such as walk/run/cycling pledges. You can set up electronic transfer of regular donations on a monthly basis.

Razoo and PayPal are just two of many ways for donors to contribute online to your organization. Causes, Crowdrise, Network for Good, and First Giving are just a few of the dozen top online fundraising sites listed by Mashable. You need to determine what method is best for your organization's online donation patterns and needs. Whatever you decide to use for online donations and sites, be sure to promote it like you would any donation opportunity!

Updating

A good tool to make it clear to viewers that this is an active website is to have something on the site that requires a date—an archive of press releases, a copyright date that changes at least annually, or a link to your blog with current entries are some ways that visitors landing on your site see that it is current.

Nothing deters a viewer faster than going to a list of events that have all already happened—if you have a long list of events, it's fine to keep the old ones on to show viewers what they missed. But once all events on the list have happened, update the list with new events, with a thank you for all who attended the past events, and start putting new events on as soon as you know when they will be. Have at least something that will show viewers that the site is being updated. If not, they will suspect that everything on the site might be old.

Marketing Your Website

Once you have created your website, don't keep it a secret! Marketing is not a dirty word just because you are a nonprofit. You need to market your organization, which often means nothing more than getting your organization out in the eyes of potential interested parties, whether they are potential donors, volunteers, or other people who would support your mission in some way. While your website may be in cyberspace, be sure your web address is on every printed piece you create for your business—letterhead, business cards, print advertisements, newsletters (print and enewsletters), radio ads—everything that has to do with your business should announce your web address. Put the address in your answering machine message. Make sure it is on the door of your storefront if you have one so anyone walking by who either doesn't have time to come in or wanders by during your off hours knows they can find you on the internet.

All of this is especially important if your web address is considerably different from your organizational name, which is not recommended but sometimes can't be avoided if another organization (or business) has already taken a web domain name similar to yours.

Your Website URL

Your website has to have a unique address, called a URL or "domain name," that will be used on the server on which it resides. Using the name of your organization is your best choice; if another business is already using the name you've chosen for your business, pick the next closest name.

Domain names must be registered for a minimum of two years, after which you can renew them. The cost to register a name for two years is quite reasonable, typically

Checklist to Get People Clicking

There's no point to having a website if you don't do what you can to get people to click on it. Here are some tips for attracting visitors, and possibly donors, members, or volunteers, to your website:

❑ Simply tell all your friends and family and ask them to tell all their friends and family.

❑ Do the appropriate search engine registration (some web services will do this for you).

❑ Every printed and online piece you send to anyone should have your website URL listed prominently.

❑ Suggest visitors bookmark your site.

❑ Trade web advertising with other websites.

❑ Create contests with giveaways that drive people to your site.

❑ Change your website content regularly to keep people coming back to see what's new.

❑ Join online discussion groups.

❑ If you do public speaking, always mention your site.

❑ Provide an "expert" column to newspapers and make sure to mention your website.

❑ Connect your website to social media links (see the social media chapter for other ideas).

These are just a few of a long list of ideas for getting people to come to your website in the first place, keep coming back, and to encourage them to tell everyone they know. Click around to websites in organizations similar to yours or in any category that interests you, see what catches your eye, and get other creative ideas to drive people to your site.

Smart Tip

Tip...

It can't be emphasized enough how useful it is to spend time looking at other organizations' websites, particularly in your category, before you design your own—whether you do it yourself or hire a designer. Keep a checklist of what you like and don't like about these websites and incorporate these findings into your design plans. Choose colors, typefaces, and other stylistic elements that work on other websites.

under $100 per name. You may want to register your name not only with the .org suffix, but register .com as well if it's available so that a for-profit business with the same name or something similar doesn't snatch it up. There are several companies that handle registration; GoDaddy and DOMAIN.com are well known.

Keep 'Em Interested

Once you get visitors checking out your site, there are some ways to keep them there as long as possible. The longer they are there, the more likely they are to look at everything you have to offer.

Be sure they know immediately what organization's website they have landed on. Make it easy for them to contact you by having a "Contact Us" button that makes it simple for them to send you a message.

Keep your website fun and changing. Do contests, include puzzles, whatever you can for fun interaction, but always connect it to your organization and its mission.

Choosing a Web Host

You must select a server to host your website. Examples of well-known web hosts include Microsoft Network, GoDaddy, and Prodigy, but there are many, many smaller hosts available.

Before choosing a web host, ask these questions:

Dollar Stretcher

Check out YahooSiteBuilder.com, Web.com, or Weebly.com for inexpensive web design solutions. Cheap or even free, these companies offer templates for website design, free domain names, and a web host site. Weebly, for instance, offers a basic template for free; more complex sites cost a fee. These sites are good for startup purposes while you get up and running and have some funding to have a site designed to exactly meet your needs.

▲

- How often does the site go down?
- How long does it take to fix the site when it goes down?
- What is its customer support system?
- How many incoming lines does the server have?
- What is the server's experience with high-traffic sites?
- How big is the server?

The price of web fame starts as low as $14.95 per month. Some of the hosts will also allow you to register your domain at the same time.

Ethical (and Legal) Concerns

A brief word on copyright, fair use, and intellectual property concerns when it comes to your website.

It is not okay to use other people's writing, articles, blurbs, photos, and/or music on your website without permission. Just because it is on your website and in cyberspace and you are not printing or selling their work does not make it okay for you to use it for free. If there is something you really want to use, that you think is perfect for your website and what you are trying to get across, by all means attempt to gain permission to use it. But if you can't figure out who owns it or can't make contact with the owner/creator, find something else, create something yourself, or hire someone to create something that you will own and can use however you would like.

Your Website Is Your Friend

Websites can do so much for so little cost and effort that it's hard to imagine how nonprofits ever survived before the consumer internet came along. Although there certainly are people out there who aren't electronically connected, given the decreasing cost of electronic devices with wireless capabilities where you can connect in a café without having to pay for internet service at home or the transformation of free libraries into electronic resource centers, almost everyone can be if they want to be. And that means that your organization can present almost everyone with a high level of high-quality information without having to print thousands of brochures or other materials. Be sure to print your web address on every business card and include it on every email, change it and update it frequently, and let it work hard for your organization.

Socially Acceptable
The Unavoidable World of Social Media

Social media, defined by Wikipedia as "media for social interaction," is no longer new, no longer avoidable, and is a proven way to get your message to the world and communicate your mission to the right audience. A lot of it is free, or practically free (don't underestimate the cost of your or a staff member's time!), so it is pretty close to a nonprofit organization's dream. Use it, use it often, and use it wisely.

The Players

LinkedIn and Facebook are old enough now that they are beginning to look like the typewriters of the social media world. New players are coming to the social media game all the time. While, as stated earlier, you should definitely use social media tools and use them often, part of using them wisely is using the ones that are right for your audience. Leave the rest for others; you don't have to use a social media tool just because it exists.

If you find it all overwhelming, there is no lack of expertise to help you sort it out. You could do something as simple as engage a highly tech-savvy high school student (read: almost any high school student) to volunteer to help you map out a social media strategy (yes, you should have a strategy; more about that later) or you could seek out workshops, seminars, webinars, and consultants—some of which are free—to help you navigate this important aspect of communication.

Enews: Traditional Media with a Digital Twist

Much of traditional media—newsletters, for example—are still used prominently in the nonprofit world. However, they are now often generated digitally and transmitted electronically—the "enewsletter"—rather than in print on paper by post. Sometimes, depending on their typical member base and their computer expertise, organizations offer their materials both ways and let the recipient decide whether to get their news in print or electronically. If your members tend to be an older audience who missed the technological explosion and wouldn't know a tweet from a pin (and don't care to know), then you will still want to offer a print newsletter. But even if that is the case, you don't have to send a print newsletter to your entire mailing list. You could sort out who does not have email and send

Smart Tip

Tip...

If you decide to send your newsletter only in electronic form to the people in your database who have email addresses but are worried that maybe they would still like the newsletter in print—ask! People loved to be asked their preferences. Many will want to save you the cost of printing and will be glad you made the switch.

print newsletters only to them while sending the newsletter electronically only to the members of your database who provide you with an email address.

Whatever you do, an enewsletter is perhaps the most basic way to communicate with members, prospective members, or anyone who provides your organization with their email address. Enewsletters take a traditional format with which most people are comfortable (the newsletter) and integrate it with the digital format that has become part of everyday life (email), delivering it to whatever electronic device on which the reader receives email, be it a desktop, laptop or tablet computer, or a phone (although if you really think your members' main electronic device is the smartphone, you will want to learn about creating a mobile version of your enewsletter or otherwise making it phone-friendly).

Netiquette

The dramatic increase in the use of email entails an understanding of good etiquette when it comes to emailing. The last thing you want to do is offend a donor or potential donor. So follow these guidelines for proper emailing:

○ Never use all uppercase letters in the body of your email or in the subject line of either your email or enews or eblast. It is considered the equivalent of shouting.

○ Spell check your emails. Just because email is quick, it doesn't have to be sloppy. It's not a problem when you are emailing with friends and family, but not professional when you are engaging donors, sponsors, and other constituents.

○ Be enticing, maybe even intriguing, but at the same time give an accurate sense of what your email is about in the subject line. If you have carefully selected people who care about your organization's mission, they will open your email.

○ Create a signature for your email so that every email you compose automatically includes your name, your title, your organization's name, address, phone number, and email address so the recipient can quickly see how to contact you.

○ Keep your messages short and to the point.

There are two key things to keep in mind about an enewsletter:

1. *Creating a newsletter is time consuming.* Just because enewsletters are cheaper to send (no printing, no mailing costs) doesn't mean you don't need to spend time pulling the newsletter content together. Think carefully about whether a newsletter at all is right for your organization and whether the time it takes to pull it together will bring you a return of equal value—that equal value may be monetary in the form of increased donations or it could be simply "donor care," letting those people who have contributed know what you are doing to further your mission with their contributions.

2. *Solicit enewsletter subscribers on your own website and at your own events.* Sending enewsletters out unsolicited is considered "spam"; spamming is not only illegal but it creates ill will with your potential customers. Always provide them an easy way to "unsubscribe" or "opt out" of your electronic mailings. But once you create a useful, readable, information-packed newsletter, people will be happy to get it.

Blasts

The so-called eblast is different from an enewsletter. Where an enewsletter should be an infrequent, regularly scheduled email full of entertaining and informative news about lots of different topics, including things that have already happened that you are simply reporting on, an eblast should be on one topic of timely importance sent at a key moment. For example, if there is a bill coming up in your state legislature that is integral to your mission and your constituents will not only want to know about it but could influence it, you could send an eblast explaining the bill, why it is important, key information like when it is going to be voted on, and a call to action telling exactly what your constituents should do to help with the outcome. (Be ever mindful, however, about the amount of this kind of advocacy your organization is allowed to do under the IRS regulations regarding public policy lobbying and advocacy for your category of organization.)

Give links to key websites or to legislator emails or whatever can help you fulfill your mission of being a watchdog for your constituents on topics that matter enough to them to be a member of or donor to your organization.

Perhaps you have a significant fundraiser coming up that your members and people on your email list would surely like to know about and perhaps attend. Let them know in a timely fashion, but don't hound them four times a week for two months about the event. Give them the info they need to learn more—your website address, a phone number, a link to buy tickets to the event right then and there—so that they feel your eblast about the event was useful to them. When you do follow-up eblasts about the event, be sure to include pertinent details that will make them feel they aren't being tormented by your eblasts but that, even if they have bought tickets already, your eblast contains information that interests them.

Perhaps you have lined up the key speaker for the event—announce that for your eblast while providing a "buy tickets" link for those who haven't made their plans to come yet. If your event has an auction component—live or silent—send out an ecommunication that tells some of the latest items that will be up for auction. Again, this entices those who haven't bought tickets yet to join in and it provides new information for those who have bought tickets already to plan for and get excited about their evening.

Some of the vehicles for creating/sending enews and eblasts are Constant Contact, MailChimp, Getresponse, and Benchmark, to name but a few, with new players entering the scene all the time. Most all have a free entry-level version that has limitations such as number of photos, templates available, and number of contacts you can send to. Then they offer differing paid levels to increase flexibility and accessibility, with the most expensive usually being the one where they create a custom design for you.

These upper levels are often not terribly expensive—but again, don't underestimate the cost of the time it takes to create all this yourself. If you love doing it, then go for it. But if you find this kind of thing supremely frustrating and/or you are super picky, the free and lower levels may just take way too much of your or a staff member's valuable time as you fuss with trying to make something perfect that can't be made the way you want it because of the limitations of the chosen template.

Press Releases

Press releases, also called "news releases," should be just that—news. If you have a piece of news to send to the media, by all means do it. A new hire, an expansion of your organization, collaboration with another organization, relocation, a significant donation, and accolades for a staff member or the organization in general are all news

Tip...

Smart Tip
Keep an archive of your news releases on your website—it's a great way for the casual browser to check out your organization's activities.

items. News sources love to get press releases via email; attachments are usually fine, and photos are typically welcome, but you should check with each individual publication you plan to send to and submit accordingly.

Event listings such as a public event you are creating are not news and should not be sent in a news release format. You can still email event listings but you should find out who the person is on the staff of newspapers and magazines that handles the event listings.

Also go online and plug your event into all the local event sites that are appropriate—there are lots of ways to get your information on the web!

Social Media

The rise of "social media" presents a fantastic opportunity for all small-business owners to meet and engage with targeted audiences full of thousands of potential customers. The cost of entry into this marketing channel is often only your time—however, don't underestimate the cost of your time! If used correctly, participating in social media will help your business grow through powerful word-of-mouth campaigns.

To get started, there are a few things you should set up right away: a Facebook page, a Twitter account, and a YouTube channel. These social media accounts will become useful tools for you to interact with your audience.

Here are eight great tips on using social media to your advantage from Jason R. Rich, author of *Start Your Own Blogging Business* (Entrepreneur Press, 2010):

1. Before you start any social media outreach, define your target audience. How old are they? Do the people in your audience tend to be more female than male? Think about the kind of people you get your message in front of—then hang out online with them.

2. Once your target audiences are defined, locate them online. Search Facebook, YouTube, Twitter, and MySpace for groups, organizations, channels, regions, or discussions that would contain the people you would like to know about your organization.

3. Use social media search and organizational tools to help you find your audiences. Some sites, like Facebook and YouTube, have great built-in search functions that will help you find your audience. To find your audience on Twitter, try using external sites like Twibes and TwittGroups.com.

4. Once you've found your audience on these sites, join their groups and lists so that you can follow the ongoing conversation. Listen and learn the etiquette and major players. Spend a week or more just following along.

5. Once you're familiar with the etiquette and people involved, jump into the conversation when and where appropriate. Do not hide who you are or the organization you represent. Become a regular voice in the conversation and offer your friendly expertise to others. Invite people back to your website and social media accounts to see what it is you do.

6. Once you're a regular voice in the conversation, don't be shy about doing a little promotion. Contests, giveaways, and raffles can be great tools for audience interaction and promotion of your organization. People will love the chance to play in your contest and will invite friends to join in the fun.

7. As your audience grows, stay creative. Invent new ways to engage your audience and encourage them to invite their friends. Avoid hard "sales pitches"—people do not forward commercials to their friends. They forward value and information.

8. Finally, do not try to do everything everywhere. Sometimes it seems there are as many social media platforms as there are websites. To try to maintain a presence on all of them is unsustainable. Focus on the top two or three that have proven to contain the largest number of people in your organization's target audience.

Help!

If it looks like you might spend all your time keeping up with Facebook, eblasts, Twitter tweets, and more, there are tools to help! Check out so-called "social media management" software such as Hootsuite, NimbleContact, or Friendly to help you manage all of the social media tools you feel like you benefit from using.

Remember, social media provides you with the opportunity to *meet* your audience—not *sell* to your audience. People

Stat Fact
The relative newcomer Pinterest caught up with Twitter by the end of 2012, with each having approximately 15 percent of U.S. internet users also using their social media, and Twitter having a slight edge over Pinterest, according to Pew Research Center.

do not join these social media networks to find marketers. They join and participate for friendly interaction and the value that that interaction adds to their day. Provide that friendly interaction in the right platforms, and you will see your audience grow.

Blogs

A *blog*, a shortened version of "web log," is a web page of typically personal and short diary-like entries that focus on a specific topic. Nonprofit organizations can make great use of blogs, garnering followers who are eager to hear personal stories within the mission (yours!) they are interested in.

Like websites, there are templates, mostly free, available to make the blogging process simple—you sign up, create your blog, write your entries, and the template sets up an archive for you. Blogspot, WordPress, and Blogger are a few more popular blog platforms. Some website creation services, like Weebly (which offers simple templates and web design services for more complicated sites as well as hosting), offer blogging as an option with your website.

You don't have to be a bestselling writer to write your own blog. But if writing really isn't even a distant strong suit for you, find someone within your organization who is a good writer or consider hiring a professional freelance writer to help you with it. Create a draft in Word, email it to your writing professional, and he or she can make it zing—and probably edit the grammar and proofread it also. It's worth the small fee that an hour or two a week (or however often you do your blog) will cost. You pay an accountant to make your numbers look right, why not pay a writer to make you sound just right to your target audience?

Try to include both pictures and perhaps links to sites with further information in your blog. Don't make your blog a strong sell; this is your chance to be personal with your constituents.

And like websites, no one will know you even have a blog unless you tell the world. Be sure to use phrases in your blog and mark keyword tags that help your blog appear when people search that word or phrase. For example, if you are blogging about the

Smart Tip

Tip...

Find an online-savvy writer who understands search engine optimization (SEO) and can write/edit your online content for all outlets using the right language to make sure that when people search a topic, your information comes up early in the list of results.

Entering the Blogosphere

Blogs are essentially online journals or brief newsletters, sometimes with more than one author. You may find blogs useful for networking, brainstorming, and simply commiserating with other nonprofit organizations. These sites allow for a back-and-forth of ideas and frustrations. Check out NonprofitMarketingBlog.com from Network for Good to not only see what blogs are all about but to get some good information to help you with your nonprofit startup, and beyond.

new seminar in good nutrition for teens, be sure to use the words "nutrition" and "teens" several times in the body of the blog.

You can link your blog to your Facebook and LinkedIn pages as well so your friends and acquaintances on those sites will know when you've published a new post on your blog. It appears with some initial teaser copy, enticing them to click on the link.

Facebook

Facebook is geared toward communicating with your network of friends. However, friends "like" websites that they want to support or really do, in fact, like. So create a Facebook page for your organization. It used to be that the Facebook community frowned on promoting with the Facebook platform, but those days are changing. With ads on Facebook and sponsored posts (where you pay a fee to have your post made prominent), Facebook users are getting well accustomed to things being promoted through this popular social media platform.

Postings to your Facebook timeline might include fun anecdotes from a recent event you held. Or you might create an event and post it to your entire list of friends, especially if many are local. Even if many aren't local, your Facebook friends like to see what your organization is up to. But don't forget that if you post pictures and name names, get permission from those in the photos or from anyone who is mentioned in an anecdote you want to tell. Just because Facebook is free does not mean it is okay to post things about other people without permission.

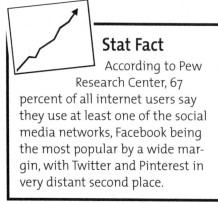

Stat Fact
According to Pew Research Center, 67 percent of all internet users say they use at least one of the social media networks, Facebook being the most popular by a wide margin, with Twitter and Pinterest in very distant second place.

Check out the Facebook pages of organizations with whom you are a member to see how they are using Facebook to their advantage. "Like" their organizational Facebook page so you will get their posts.

LinkedIn

LinkedIn is thought of as the Facebook of the business world. The general advice is to make your LinkedIn page more formal than a Facebook page might be. This is not where you will list events and post fun anecdotes and photos of events you've held. Here you're presenting your mission statement, your vision statement, and an outline of the good work that your organization is doing.

This is where you gain business contacts, where potential board members, large donors, and others check out your organization. LinkedIn is very business-oriented and is a good place to "link up" with the connections of your connections.

Twitter

A Twitter account for your business may be best used as an extension of a blog. You can send quick messages of up to 140 characters, a "tweet," to your subscribers. Twitter is particularly useful if your organization has a big project underway, a capital campaign, or is building a new facility and you want to keep donors up to date on progress.

Smart Tip

Tip...

Twitter—whose tweets can only be 140 characters or fewer—is a more casual and personal media outlet like a blog and is referred to as a *microblog*.

Instagram

Although it's been around a while, Instagram, a photo-focused social media outlet self-described as a "fun and quirky way to share your life with friends through a series of photos," is still not anywhere near as popular as Facebook, Twitter, LinkedIn, or

Pinterest. Instagram is available through the Apple App and Google Play stores for free; there are no current plans to develop it for other platforms such as Windows or Android until they feel they have the Apple and Google platforms solid.

Take a picture, use one of Instagram's filters to enhance your photo, then post it on Instagram for your followers to view. Instagram photos can be shared to other social media sites as well, such as Facebook.

The benefits of the use of Instagram by most nonprofits is probably minimal at best at this early stage. An organization that does a lot of outdoor work and work in the field might find it useful for keeping followers engaged with the work of the organization. However, as mentioned before, carefully consider adding to your social media needs until you have determined that the outlet has a specific benefit to your organization's ability to accomplish its mission.

Tumblr

Owned by Yahoo!, Tumblr is a microblogging (short post or "tumblelog") platform—somewhere in between Twitter's 140-character "tweets" and a regular blog. As with regular long-form blogs, you can create posts and schedule them to release over a period of time. As of August 2013, Tumblr is reported to be hosting over 130 million blogs. Wow, that's a lot of blogging! Clearly, if you aren't on the blog bandwagon, it might be time since lots of others are finding it useful.

More social media outlets are coming down the pike every week. The important thing to keep in mind is to use the ones that work best for your organization. Don't let your organization get overwhelmed feeling like you have to be involved in all of them. You exist to fulfill your mission, and it's unlikely that your mission is to use as much social media as possible.

Social Media Strategy

So now you know about all these great social media platforms—and more are on the way almost every day. But, as is the case

Tip...

Smart Tip
Make sure to prominently list your events on your own website and feed them out in your other social media outlets while posting them on other websites where applicable.

with most nonprofit organizations, you are already seriously overwhelmed with more to do than can possibly be done in a day. How to add something like keeping current on social media postings to your organization's plate?

One way to keep up with all this social media activity, besides using one of the social media organizing tools, is to divide the platforms among your staff, if you have staff yet. Take care of Twitter posts yourself, let your communications manager update the website, while someone in your development department keeps the Facebook page current. If your administrative assistant is a great writer, give him the task of doing a weekly blog. Keep everyone apprised of what everyone else is doing with their social media task with either a list of topics, or add social media to your weekly staff meeting. It not only helps everyone figure out what to post this week but it also helps everyone work together for your social media to be a well-blended part of getting the work of your organization out there in cyberspace.

If you don't have staff, reach out to the board and to volunteers with writing skills who you trust to run everything by you before posting.

Get Social

Social media has saturated almost all the world yet is still young enough to be in a constant state of flux. Don't try to do it all, but do pick a couple outlets that work best for your organization.

Sustainability and Growth
Keeping Things Going

Your nonprofit is up and running. You have systems in place, programs are up and running. Where do you go from here?

▲

Strategic Plan

A key tool for knowing the answer to that question is the strategic plan. Hopefully you did one before you started your organization. But strategic plans, while not exactly dynamic, should be consistently updated.

Time Frame

A logical time frame for a strategic plan for a small nonprofit is three years. Year one would contain a lot of detail about the organization's plans for the immediate future. Years two and three would have increasingly less detail. You might even add a couple of general comments at the end of a three-year strategic plan about years four and five.

As far as time frame for completion of the plan, as a startup, this is the first strategic plan you will create as an organization so don't rush it. If it takes six months or a year to create your strategic plan, that's fine—take the time it needs for everyone to participate and buy in to the plan.

Logistics

The board and executive director are the key drivers for the strategic plan. This is a great opportunity for a joint effort by the whole board.

Consider having a consultant serve as an unbiased facilitator who can take the board through a constructive process. You may want to hold a session where you come up with the key goals for the organization for the next three years. You will likely come up with many more than you will want to include in your strategic plan; then work your way back to a manageable number of goals.

At your next meeting, take each goal (you may want more than one meeting for this step, depending on how many goals you have) and brainstorm all the possible strategies for that goal to be met. You might want to talk about the resources needed to accomplish this goal at this stage or you may want to wait until you have this part of the document finalized before attaching numbers.

Next, break the plan down into a manageable project by having each piece taken on by a board member to create the narrative for the goal for the plan, pulling in the brainstorming lists from the work sessions. The rest of the process can be done within the time frame of regular board meetings if you take one goal at a time. The executive director and board president or key board member of the goal can hammer out the details of the goal narrative before circulating it to the whole board in advance of the meeting in which it will be discussed and finalized.

Lastly, once you have gone through all the goals this way, pull them all together into a great strategic plan document.

Getting It Done

Once you have the strategic plan for your organization, it is time to attach a work plan to each of the goals, and the strategies you have recognized to accomplish them. Be realistic based on your organization's ability and personnel that will enable you to get things done.

For each goal and each strategy, figure out what needs to be done to accomplish it. Do you need volunteers to help get it done? Where are the resources for this project coming from? Is a program attached to the goal that will bring in income specifically targeted to the goal?

Revisit

Once your strategic plan document is "finished," don't tuck it away and consider it "done." This is a working document that the board and director should be referring to regularly and becoming very familiar with. Decision-making in board meetings can be informed by what is in the strategic plan.

Your strategic plan should be included in the packet for every new board member. The board worked hard to create this document; use it as the guide it is intended to be.

Topics for Strategic Plan

Identity

Do you feel like your nonprofit could use a stronger profile in your target community? Nonprofits, like any business, can experience a surge of publicity at startup. The media by nature gravitates toward the new.

One way to work on your identity is to think about what your organization's identity actually is. Do you have a strong logo that is associated with your organization? Think the red cross of the American Red Cross. Most drivers can recognize the logo of a car brand while driving down the road. Your identity doesn't have to be represented just by a graphic brand. LiveStrong usurped the color yellow with their logo color and yellow wrist bands. Brands are strengthened using mascots—think Geico's gecko or Smokey Bear of the U.S. Forest Service.

You can try to up your brand identity yourself, but there are graphic design firms out there that specialize in creating branding campaigns. Some will work for nonprofits at a substantially reduced rate or even pro bono.

Search for grant possibilities that would help with raising a nonprofit's profile. For a modest amount of money, a brand identity campaign can bring substantial return for the investment. Consider whether this is a worthwhile thing to focus on in your strategic plan.

Physical Plant

If your organization owns a building, you may need to address the maintenance, renovation, restoration, or expansion of that building in your strategic plan. Buildings represent a large expenditure for an organization; they are also an asset and assets need to be protected and cared for.

While they are a lot of care and sometimes headache, buildings also can represent incredible opportunities for sustainability. As owner, you can lease part of the building, expand to add retail space where you had none, renovate to create a classroom for giving workshops—the possibilities are only limited by your imagination and your ability to find the funding to accomplish that goal.

> ### Smart Tip
> The "strategic" part of this planning process is the continual attention to current changes in the organization and its external environment, and how this affects the future of the organization.
>
> —Free Management Library, ManagementHelp.org

The upshot is, if you are going to own a building, why not look at it as not only an asset in and of itself, but as a key part of your future. Including a "physical plant" goal in your strategic plan will allow you to do just that.

Engagement

What goal might you list in your strategic plan that would ramp up the engagement in your organization? Think about other groups or interests that mesh with yours—and don't be ashamed to fabricate an engagement opportunity. Do snowmobilers use the mountain biking trails you are trying to create? Can you mount an exhibit at your art museum that focuses on animals? Can you offer some cooking classes at your appliance museum and pull in the foodie crowd? If you are helping children not go hungry, is there a way to engage their moms that you aren't doing yet?

Your strategic plan might have a more general goal that states that you want to "engage two new categories of constituents." Constantly finding new groups to be interested in your organization can be a huge foundation for growth. These are the people who turn into members, event attendees, and general donors.

Finances

There are not many nonprofits who shouldn't put "improving financial position" in their strategic plan. But your strategic plan should be more specific than that. What part of your finances need the most improvement? Should your strategic plan goal focus on cash flow? Or donations? More specifically, does your annual fund need improvement? Perhaps the retail store is not performing as it might.

Finances will almost always make sense to be a part of the strategic plan. But narrow it down to what kind of finances, what kind of improvements, and you will have a more useful goal for your strategic planning process.

Hiring

Believe it or not, hiring can be a critical part of sustainability and growth. Not only is having more employees a sign of growth of some kind, but strategic employees will actually help your organization grow.

What key positions could your organization make use of to allow you to expand your programming to enable you to offer more in the accomplishment of your mission? Don't forget that actual donations or fees aren't the only way to make an employee worth their salary. Nonprofits should always be thinking about how to better accomplish their mission, which is what potential donors and grant funders want to see. Although they all want you to be doing things that bring in income to sustain your operation, funders and donors aren't interested in how much money you make, but how much you are able to make an impact on your organizational mission.

Capital Campaign Time?

A capital campaign is another way to move your organization to the next level. Capital campaigns are often initiated for building projects. However, they can be used to create an endowment, an operating reserve, or toward a significant new programming initiative. Comprehensive capital campaigns can do all three at once.

Think through what your organization may need for a large monetary investment.

> **Smart Tip**
>
> Collect case statements from other organizations whenever you can. Keeping a sample collection of other organizations' fundraising appeals and campaigns is a useful collection to have.

Case Statement

A capital campaign of any kind typically starts with a case statement—a collection of information that outlines why the organization is ready for this kind of investment and why what you plan to do with the money is needed at this time. That is, you make your case for support.

A case statement should include some history of your organization (which, for a startup, is a little short). Information about the board, director, and founder's history, experience, and anything related to their ability to accomplish the mission could offset historical information by including all this background in support of the organization's capabilities.

The case statement should also include information about the project you are initiating the capital campaign for. Any valid, up-to-date statistics that support the need should be included. If there are appropriate images, include those. And be sure to explain how the campaign benefits the donor you are reaching out to.

While you don't want to look extravagant or spend a lot of money, your case statement materials should look professional. This is a reflection on the professionalism of the organization, which reflects back on your ability to accomplish what you are setting out to do.

Growing Too Fast

One cautionary tale from the for-profit world is the problem with growing too fast. Growing to expand your services and widen the reach of your mission is admirable and something to work toward. But it's important to do this within the organization's ability to keep up.

If you are not prepared physically—office space, capacity of your soup kitchen, museum, or animal shelter—you could find yourself quickly overwhelmed and unable to provide the service you've been providing all along with any quality.

Also, do you have the right person at the helm for significant growth? If not, can the person in place get the training that would make him or her the right person? Additional employees are often a necessity with growth, but they come with a lot of additional concerns beyond just extra salary expenses—office space, human resources needs, and compensation expectations beyond salary.

Growing is great but think it through very carefully. If an opportunity arises to become exponentially larger, reach more constituents, and greatly expand your ability to accomplish your mission, be sure you are ready. Many a for-profit company went under because it "grew too fast." Nonprofits can experience the same problem, perhaps even more easily. Having all the ducks that we've covered in this book in row—strategic plan, succession plan, capital campaign strategy—you can be ready to make a giant step into the next phase of your nonprofit's life.

Appendix A
Sample Strategic Plan

The Appliance Museum
Strategic Plan 2020–2023

Mission

To preserve and display one example of common kitchen household appliances for future generations.

Vision

That all generations appreciate the ingenuity, life-changing convenience, and design innovations represented by the common household appliance.

Background

The Appliance Museum was the brainchild of four New England women (see bios below) who realized that the household kitchen appliance, both large and small, was a game changer for families during the early years of these inventions and throughout history have been reinvented and adapted to the changing culture of family life, manufacturing capabilities, and technological advances.

With this in mind, the four founders began collecting appliances. This collection is currently scattered around storage units in four different states. The founders have established nonprofit status for the museum and now have a site on which they are planning a facility that will allow appropriate display space and will have interpretive signage and changing exhibits. The organization has launched the silent stage of a capital campaign to construct the building.

GOAL ONE
Finish Capital Campaign, $1,200,000
($500,000 already raised) by end of 2020

Strategy 1: Research and apply for grants that fund capital campaigns, goal $100,000.

Strategy 2: Launch "Appliance Hall of Fame" name plaques, $500 each, sell 200, $100,000.

Strategy 3: Mail mass appeal, raise $100,000.

Strategy 4: Secure corporate donor(s), $200,000.

Strategy 5: Personal cultivation of several donors with capacity: $200,000.

Resources needed: $18,000 (15 percent of fundraising goal) for mailings, lunches, and case statement printing.

GOAL TWO
Build Museum Facility (by end of 2021)

Strategy 1: Complete donated land transaction.

Strategy 2: Design facility (currently underway with donated architectural work by board member).

Strategy 3: Construct and furnish building, move artifacts.

GOAL THREE
Create a Marketing Plan (concurrent with building facility)

Strategy 1: Create printed piece to mail about opening of museum.

Strategy 2: Design and print rack cards for tourism racks throughout region.

Strategy 3: Expand existing website to reflect opening of museum.

Strategy 4: Create social media marketing plan.

GOAL FOUR
Formulate a Strong Visitor Experience

Strategy 1: Work with museum display expert to create a strong visitor experience with interactive exhibits.

Strategy 2: Create exhibits specific to children to engage school field trips.

Strategy 3: Secure grant to have introductory video created for greeting area.

Strategy 4: Order inventory and open museum store.

Appendix B
Resources for Nonprofits

They say you can never be too rich or too thin. While those points could be argued, we believe you can never have too many resources. Therefore, we present for your consideration a some sources for you to check into, check out, and harness for your own personal information blitz.

These sources are tidbits, ideas to get you started on your research. They are by no means the only sources out there, and they should not be taken as the "Ultimate Answer." We have done our research, but businesses tend to move, change, fold, and expand. As we have repeatedly stressed, do your homework. Get out and start investigating.

Associations

Center for Nonprofit Success
Washington, D.C.
(202) 469-6773
cfnps.org

This group's mission is to provide training, knowledge, and resources to help nonprofits succeed, including mentoring, workshops, a job bank, consulting, and research.

Corporation for National & Community Service
Nationalservice.gov

Covering AmeriCorps, SeniorCorps, and much else concerning volunteering in the United States. The site includes statistics about volunteering and information about current initiatives like First Lady Michelle Obama's Let's Read, Let's Move, and Martin Luther King's Day of Service.

National Council of Nonprofits
1200 New York Avenue NW, Suite 700
Washington, DC 20005
(202) 962-0322
councilofnonprofits.org

Largest network of nonprofits in the United States. The organization serves as a champion for nonprofits, advocating at the state legislative level.

Society for Nonprofits
P.O. Box 510354
Livonia, MI 48151
snpo.org

The Society for Nonprofits (snpo.org) was formed in 1983. Membership includes access to their many publications including the magazine *Nonprofit World*; weekly grants email update, GrantStation Insider; and the bi-monthly enewsletter Nonprofit Currents.

State Organizations

Find your state organization at the National Council of Nonprofits website, which lists the nonprofit associations in 36 states at http://www.councilofnonprofits.org/find-your-state-association

Urban Institute
2100 M Street N.W.
Washington, D.C. 20037
Urban.org

The Urban Institute "gathers data, conducts research, evaluates programs, offers technical assistance overseas, and educates Americans on social and economic issues—to foster sound public policy and effective government. The Urban Institute builds knowledge about the nation's social and fiscal challenges, practicing open-minded, evidence-based research to diagnose problems and figure out which policies and programs work best, for whom, and how." The brainchild of President Johnson, who saw a need for a nonpartisan group to analyze the problems in that America's urban areas faced, this is the place to go for analysis of public policy and programs and statistics on the nonprofit sector.

Books

Entrepreneur Press and Rich Mintzer, *Start Your Own Grant-Writing Business: Your Step-by-Step Guide to Success.* (Irvine, CA: Entrepreneur Press, 2013)

Grace, Kay Sprinkel. *The Ultimate Board Member's Book, Newly Revised Edition: A 1-Hour Guide to Understanding and Fulfilling Your Role and Responsibilities.* (Medfield, MA: Emerson & Church Publishers, 2013)

Neef, David J., and Randall C. Moss. *The Future of Nonprofits: Innovate and Thrive in the Digital Age.* (Hoboken, NJ: John Wiley & Sons, 2011)

O'Connell, Brian. *The Board Member's Book: Second Edition.* (New York, NY: The Foundation Center, 1993)

Pakroo, Peri H., J.D. *Starting & Building a Nonprofit: A Practical Guide: 4th Edition.* (Berkeley, CA: Nolo Press, 2011)

Penna, Robert M., Ph.D. *The Nonprofit Outcomes Toolbox: A Complete Guide to Program Effectiveness, Performance Measurements, and Results.* (Hoboken, NJ: John Wiley & Sons, 2011)

Roeger, Katie L., Amy S. Blackwood, and Sarah L. Pettijohn. *The Nonprofit Almanac, 2012.* (Washington, D.C.: Urban Institute Press, 2012)

Magazines

The Nonprofit Times
thenonprofittimes.com
Billed as "the leading business publication for nonprofit management."

The Chronicle of Philanthropy
philanthropy.com
This magazine contains everything you want to know about philanthropy and a lot you wouldn't even think to ask. It even has cartoons!

Websites

Achieve (AchieveGuidance.com). Design and creative services to help build awareness for nonprofit causes

Council on Foundations (cof.org). Provides links to other sites such as government grant sources and private sector foundations

Grantsalert (GrantsAlert.com). Started in 1996, GrantsAlert helps teachers and schools with grants. The site offers education on writing grants, how to find grants, and the latest updates on education-related grants.

Nonprofit Finance Fund (NonprofitFinanceFund.org). Financial advisory services

Nolo.com. Legal advice for for-profits, nonprofits, and individuals

Fundraising Coach (FundraisingCoach.com). Expert nonprofit fundraising training, seminars, and webinars

Glossary

Here are some terms that you will encounter as you become involved in the nonprofit world. Some of the words are common words that are used in unique ways in the nonprofit arena.

Acknowledgment: The follow-up thank-you letter sent after a donation is made to the organization is also known as an "acknowledgment," acknowledging the gift in a way that can be used by the donor in reporting to the IRS.

Capacity: A common term in nonprofits that can refer to two things: 1) how much a potential donor is capable of giving based on a calculation using knowledge of income, assets, and other anecdotal knowledge, and 2) the number of constituents an organization can serve. "Capacity building" refers to doing things that allow the

▲

organization to serve more constituents. Constituents can be members or visitors to a museum or number of people you can serve at a soup kitchen.

Capital campaign: When an organization needs a large amount of money for a specific reason, they can launch a "capital campaign"—essentially a specific campaign to raise money. A capital campaign may be launched to construct a building, raise money to create an endowment, renovate an existing building, or create a major program. "Comprehensive capital campaign" may be launched to fund several of these things.

Database: Database in the nonprofit world is typically specific to donors. While these databases keep track of donations and can compile financial listings, they are designed to focus on donors, not numbers. Donor records can link to relationships with other records in your database, can keep track of spouses and children, assign a steward to the donor, and note any contact that has been had with the donor.

Development: Where "development" in the for-profit world often refers to "building up"—e.g., new business development—the term "development" in a nonprofit organization refers to fundraising (a different kind of "building up"). The development office runs the logistics of the fundraising efforts that the organization makes. This is one of those terms that holds little meaning for those outside the industry and when used with the general public often needs explanation.

Donation: Donations are the gifts of cash, goods, or services given to a nonprofit organization for which nothing has been given in return. Donations are typically tax deductible. Donations that come with a gift (like a mug for your $60 donation) are only tax deductible minus the value of the gift.

Donor: A "donor" is anyone who donates to your organization, either money or services or goods. Donors can be broken down into "individuals," "corporate" or "business," and "foundations" (grant funders).

Earned income: Income from things like purchases of ball caps with the organization's name on them, items in a gift store, or fees for workshops or classes are referred to as "earned income."

Engage: When people are encouraged to donate to an organization and participate in the activities of the organization, it is commonly referred to as "engagement." Engagement can be as a volunteer, as a donor, or just someone who signs up and comes to one of your workshops or programs. Engaging people in your organization in any way is often the first step in their becoming long-term members, donors, and/or volunteers. Engagement is a way for them to learn about and appreciate what your organization does.

Foundation: A foundation is a financial entity established to hold an investment that is designed so that a certain portion of the investment's income—and sometimes a portion of the investment itself—is given away each year to charitable organizations within the interest areas of the foundation's founder(s). Directories are available, both on and offline, that keep track of foundations, how to contact them, what they fund, their guidelines, and their deadlines for applications.

Gift pyramid: For any defined campaign to raise money, a gift pyramid is created. The top of the pyramid represents the largest donors, which will also be the fewest donors. The donor pool increases in size and decreases in per-donor gift until your total goal is represented. For example, a gift pyramid for a $100,000 goal might show one $25,000 donor at the peak, two $10,000 donors in the next layer, four $5,000 donors in the next layer, six $2,500 donors, ten $1,000 donors, and at the last layer, 40 donors of varying amounts under $1,000. This gives a framework within which to place your donors as you find and get them.

Grant: A grant is an amount of money typically allocated through an application process that is awarded to the applicants that the grant funder's governing board deems worthy of funding at that moment in time. Grants range from a few hundred dollars to hundreds of thousands of dollars.

Impact: Impact is what your organization is doing to help the constituents served by your mission. An animal shelter may have an impact on reducing animal cruelty in their area of service; the avenue to that impact may be through humane education classes in the school systems and the impact statistics may be calculated by working with local law enforcement to track the reduction in cruelty cases in a certain area since your program began. Impact statistics are helpful in writing grant applications and backing up the value of your service.

In-kind donation: An in-kind donation is the donation of goods or services that you need. If you are building a new soup kitchen, the local construction company might donate their services laying the foundation. If the concrete company donates the concrete used in the foundation, that would be a donation of goods. These donations are tax deductible like any other. They should be recorded in your database and your bookkeeping software since they represent value to the organization.

Member: Many nonprofit organizations offer membership. For a few dollars, a person becomes a member. Some organizations have an active membership with an annual meeting and the membership even approves of new members of the board of directors. Some organizations offer membership that is not active but members receive benefits like discounted prices on items in your retail store, entry to your museum, or discounted fees for workshops. Donor databases will keep track of membership and help organize renewal mailings.

Moves management: This is a very nonprofit-specific term that refers to the actions taken to move a donor up the ladder of donation. For example, someone may first encounter your organization by attending an event you put on. A few months later, they may respond to an appeal you send at the holidays. A few months after that, they may become an individual member and perhaps move their membership level up over the next couple years. Ultimately, they may become a sustaining donor, making a monthly donation deducted directly from their credit card or checking account. A few years into their engagement with your organization, they may donate a large sum to a major campaign with their final move being a donation from having named you as a beneficiary of their estate.

Nonprofit: A nonprofit organization is one that, in return for tax-free status, serves a community. Myriad types of service exist, from helping low-income families, providing shelter for women suffering from abuse, providing hot meals for seniors, preserving historical resources, housing an art collection—the list is endless. Religious nonprofits make up a large percentage of the nonprofits in the United States; they are unique in and of themselves and are not covered specifically in this book.

Philanthropy: *Merriam-Webster* defines "philanthropy" as "goodwill to fellow members of the human race, especially an active effort to promote human welfare." People who are frequent or large donors to charitable causes are referred to as "philanthropic."

Proposal: A proposal in the nonprofit arena is typically referring to a grant proposal. This is an application written to a grant funder outlining a specific purpose for requesting funding and making a case for the project and for the validity and capability of the organization making the request.

Prospect: A prospect is a person who has been targeted as being a potential donor to the organization. A "qualified" prospect is one whose background shows that they both have an inclination toward charitable giving (demonstrated by evidence they have given to nonprofit organizations in the past) and have the financial capacity to give.

Volunteer: Anyone who donates time to your organization is a volunteer. Volunteers can help at an event, help in the office, or spend time helping with programs. The board of directors are all volunteers.

Webinar: Webinars are a great way to learn about specific aspects of running a nonprofit organization that can be done on your own time schedule, often for free or at least very inexpensively. Webinars abound in topics like fundraising, board work, and managing volunteers.

Index